THE PRINCIPLES OF RUGBY FOOTBALL

A Manual for Coaches and Referees

THE PRINCIPLES OF RUGBY FOOTBALL

A Manual for Coaches and Referees

Based on papers delivered at the Welsh
Rugby Union Centenary International
Conference for Coaches and Referees

London
GEORGE ALLEN & UNWIN
Boston   Sydney

George Allen & Unwin (Publishers) Ltd,
40 Museum Street, London WC1A 1LU, UK

George Allen & Unwin (Publishers) Ltd,
Park Lane, Hemel Hempstead, Herts HP2 4TE, UK

Allen & Unwin Inc.,
9 Winchester Terrace, Winchester, Mass 01890, USA

George Allen & Unwin Australia Pty Ltd,
8 Napier Street, North Sydney, NSW 2060, Australia

First published in 1983

British Library Cataloguing in Publication Data
Dawes, John
    The Principles of rugby football.
1. Rugby football coaching – Congresses
I. Title
796.33'3'07   GV945.75

ISBN 0-04-7960671

Set in 10 on 11 point Times by Rowland Phototypesetting Limited,
and printed in Great Britain
by Butler & Tanner Ltd, Frome and London

Contents

Preface

In 1980–81 the Welsh Rugby Union celebrated its Centenary. It was the last of the Home Countries to do so and therefore had a wonderful opportunity to gain from the experience of England, Scotland and Ireland. One of the most enterprising features was to hold an International Conference for Coaches and Referees. This turned out to be one of the highlights of the Centenary Year. Eighty-one countries were invited to send delegates and it was rewarding to find that well over half accepted the invitation.

The papers delivered at the Conference are here published at the request of the delegates because the contents are of immense value. They have been amended so that law changes etc can be taken into consideration, and have been edited where necessary to convert them from the spoken to the printed word, but basically they have been reproduced as delivered by the individual speakers.

At the end of the Conference the delegates were given the opportunity to make recommendations. This they did and it is appropriate to print their recommendations as an appendix to this book.

Those present at the Conference will remember the papers, but it is important for rugby men the world over to read them. The speakers have produced a wonderful manual and the WRU are grateful both to them and to the delegates for producing a Conference worthy of its Centenary.

JOHN DAWES
Coaching Organiser, WRU

Foreword

by CLIFF JONES

Cliff Jones, OBE, was President of the Welsh Rugby Union during its Centenary Year, 1980–81

Reading this book, I am aware that I am in the presence of some of the greatest thinkers about, and the greatest contributors to, rugby football in the world today. I doubt if in any other sport so many experts in their respective fields of coaching, refereeing and technical administration have ever been gathered under one roof as the contributors to this book were for the WRU Centenary International Conference for Coaches and Referees. They paid us in Wales the supreme compliment by their efforts to join us in this unique and exceptional way, and we are deeply grateful to them for all their efforts. The sum total of the experience and knowledge that these writers have to offer is truly immense.

I am particularly pleased that the book, like the Conference, is not confined solely to coaches but embraces the activities of the one man who has the profound responsibility of controlling the game – the referee. I found out after my playing days just how difficult it is to be 'the man in the middle'. A match had been arranged between the British Army of the Rhine and the Kiwis in the Hamburg Bowl in Germany in 1946. The British referee (I believe he was a Welshman from Neath) failed to arrive and at five to three our BAOR dressing-room door burst open and in tripped Brigadier Andrews, the manager of the Kiwis, followed by Charlie Saxton, their captain, and Freddie Allen, their vice-captain. 'We've had a quick pow-wow,' they said to me. The referee hasn't come, but we're quite happy for you to referee.' So I refereed reluctantly in battle-dress and when the game was over, a signal honour was conferred upon me by Brigadier Andrews personally as he pinned the coveted silver fern-leaf to my chest with the words, 'I give you this for being the worst referee we've met, not only in Great Britain but the whole of bloody Europe!'

Neither the Centenary Conference nor this book would have

been possible without the Coaching Staff of the Welsh Rugby Union, my colleagues in coaching, the Referees' Society and all those responsible for arranging such an attractive and impressive programme.

1

Introduction

by A. R. DAWSON

An outstanding former player and current world administrator, Ronnie Dawson made 28 appearances for Ireland as hooker and led his country, province and club. A regular Barbarian, he led the club to victory against the 1961 Springboks. He was captain of the British Lions in 1959 and coach to the 1968 side. On retirement he entered administration, serving on the committees of his club, province and National Union since 1970. Elected to the International Board in 1975, he is now recognised as one of the leading students of the game both technically and administratively.

My purpose in this Introduction is to dwell on some generalities about rugby football which I believe to be important and which I intend to divide into three sections: the playing, teaching and coaching of the game, refereeing; and some remarks on administration.

There has in recent times been an unprecedented explosion in the game's popularity, possibly more than in any other sport. Even more countries are now playing the game and there is a vast increase everywhere in the number and the size of clubs. This is partly because of new laws which favour attacking rugby, but can also be put down to an extension in the coverage of rugby football by radio and television. It is a well-publicised game now, and with the good publicity comes the bad. There are tremendous responsibilities, therefore, on all connected with the game: players, selectors, coaches, referees and administrators.

There are other influences on the game of rugby. Many sociological factors are changing our way of life, as well as all sport. Club players, as amateurs, have other responsibilities:

they always had to work, but the companies they work for now are demanding more from them. There is also the emphasis on family life; even compared with the 'fifties, many rugby players now are married a lot earlier and have families to look after. There are the impositions of tours – these are very desirable and sought after by players but again, a perspective is required.

Recent law-changes have certainly made the game much faster and demand more from players at all levels. Never forget that players are the life-blood of the game and that consideration has to be shown for them. They are amateurs and they have other things to do. True, the real pressure comes to relatively few men when one considers the hundreds of thousands of players of the game throughout the world, but we must recognise that those few players at top level do come under tremendous pressure. It starts at the bigger clubs and for players who go on to provincial, county and International level, the demands become almost intolerable. The best players are always wanted by their clubs, they are wanted by each of the other levels I have mentioned, they are sought after for interviews, they come under scrutiny because many of the things that happen in rugby these days, even if they have probably always happened, are now spotlighted by the eye of television. This pressure has got to be recognised by coaches, selectors and administrators. There has got to be a lot more tolerance of the pressure on top players and they should not be asked to do three or four things for rugby in a week.

The way in which young players are brought into the game is most important. Years ago, dedicated men taught much fewer players not only how to play the game but how to enjoy it and how to develop their own skills. This is not possible any more, but there have been tremendous advances through the evolution of a mini-rugby game. Now I am convinced of the virtues of introducing young boys to the game through a reduced number of players. There have been disagreements as to whether you play with five players, seven players, nine players or twelve players – why not play with the lot at different stages of the development so long as the basic skills are being properly taught? It is one of the banes of my life to see thirty eight-year-olds swarming around a field like locusts after the big fella who is carrying the ball. They are learning nothing, but it is easier for the guy who has put his trousers in his socks and gone out to work with them and blow a whistle: he puts in the time and goes away, but it is doing nothing for the introduction of the game to young people.

Between the ages of eight and twelve it is pointless having competitions. They should be outlawed by National Unions, yet they exist. Let soccer give them jerseys and cups and competitions – it doesn't matter. We have got to resist this temptation and try to teach young people the game – how to enjoy it and how to develop themselves as players. At that age it is all about teaching them how to play and discovering their game.

Those same boys, as they grow older, will have to work for exams now – my generation was probably the last which could slide into something doing nothing – and the whole structuring of schools, which in earlier days were crucial agents for introducing boys into the game, has changed. No rugby club, no rugby union can now afford just to depend on a guaranteed feed of young players into the game. We all have to work at it, and the French have set a tremendous example. The schools system does not apply there so much, but no club is allowed to play in the French Championship unless it has an approved youth section. This has to be right. It certainly gives responsibility and awareness to everybody that the feed will come through only by your own endeavours.

I make no apology for saying constantly since I came into coaching that the basic skills are the most vital element that you can have in this game. Unless they are taught early, it gets increasingly difficult to teach them later on, and impossible to teach old dogs new tricks. No matter the size of the country or the number of players, it's not on to ask national coaches to teach players at International level basic skills. It is absolutely essential that they are taught early.

Coaching is a means to an end and not an end in itself; 'success through simplicity', an understanding and a simple approach, has got to be one of the main keynotes of this whole playing exercise. Just think of the sort of vogue things that have become clichés in recent years. The hooker throwing the ball into the lineout – why? Because someone did it, everyone did it. It may be good, and I'm not questioning that it is good, but what if the hooker is not very skilful at throwing the ball into the lineout? Again, the lineout peel was a magnificent tactical innovation, probably developed to its purest form by the French in the 'fifties and 'sixties, but in Britain we copied it slavishly, we did it badly, we spent hours and hours practising it and defence against it. Other things were left alone. Then there are miss-moves in midfield: how many times have you seen teams at all levels practising and shouting and calling moves where they miss out a centre and give

3

it to a full-back coming in? There are three or four variations of it, all excellent provided that they are done at the correct time, when the players on the field decide they should be done and not when somebody off the field suggests that they might be done. And now we have the rolling maul. Again, this is a tremendous tactic, but let's not have it as a cliché and everybody at all levels trying rolling mauls.

These few examples are all excellent innovations in the game, but they must be understood and be applied out of the game, not imposed on it. No man can decide what he is going to do, certainly not a threequarter, until he gets the ball in his hands. If a move is called before the ball goes into the set piece, and it is not on when the outside-half gets it, the backs should recognise that and act accordingly.

Years ago, Australia, South Africa and New Zealand developed tremendously strong forward play. British teams just could not match it – it was too good. But in certain countries the game was built around this forward strength, possibly – I'm not saying certainly – to the detriment of back play. Likewise, there were teams on this side of the world who had some star backs but did not know how to get the ball; they just wondered why the countries from the Southern hemisphere were doing so well in their development. So there was a change, a reversal. Everybody in the early 'sixties started on unit skills, team organisation, the set scrum, how do we get the ball because if we don't get the ball we can't play rugby. That worked, so much so that during the 1980 Lions tour of South Africa it was strange to see a South African forward pack from those great days of forward play slide just a little. Yet even though the Lions won the ball, what did they do with it? They played at times into the hands of the opposition by over-doing things up front and forgetting that the timing of when you give the ball is of vital consequence. Again, it's absolutely full marks to the South African team for adapting quickly, seeing the error that was being made, bringing the defence into the right position, countering it and winning by taking opportunities and by strong good running.

So what, in general terms, should coaching be concerned with? In my opinion it is concerned with how and when things should be done, either by an individual or by the team. It is concerned with how to stand back and to observe and analyse so that one can be of assistance, how to develop the best attitudes towards the game by individuals and by the team, how to communicate all these things to the players (this is vital), how to work with the captain on tactics and how to be of assistance to him in working things out for the good of his team. Coaches *must* adopt a positive approach to the game and to training. A coach has got to build confidence in the players he is dealing with and try to remove a fear of not winning, which is the way I would prefer to put that phrase.

We have not seen on the International stage many great captains in recent years (Graham Mourie of New Zealand is a particular exception to this), but remember that it is at the peril of the game that we forget the captain, as I believe we have forgotten him to a large extent in many countries.

The reason why we fall back on the clichés that I referred to earlier is that there is at the moment far too much bad coaching. We have all been responsible for it – nobody is free from it. So coaches have to constantly re-examine themselves, what the hell they are doing and what they are trying to do. I have heard it said by a top International, whom I respect a lot, that coaching is an abomination. You have got to listen to this, and if it is bad coaching, he is probably correct.

Moving now to refereeing, it is a thankless job but one which is absolutely vital to the game. They did start off the game without any referee, back in the dark ages, but I hate to think what it would be like now without one. The one point I would like to make, and I'm sure the referees understand this just as well as I do, is that a knowledge of the game is probably even more important than a knowledge of the laws. Of course the laws have to be known, but if you know the law-book backwards and don't know the game, if you don't know what the players are trying to do and have no feeling for the game, then the quality not only of refereeing but of the game will suffer. Each National Union usually has a Referees' Society or Association and in turn each province or district has a Referees' Association to work out and develop the laws, arrange the administration of referees, referee the games etc. There is a danger here that the refereeing set-up can become slightly divorced from the National Union itself; everyone is too busy and there are so many things to be done. But at no stage can refereeing be divorced and I welcome the fact that this book brings together all aspects of the game.

The International Board are constantly looking at the laws of the game, and in my opinion changing far too much too often. It is vitally important that each National Union, with its referees, fully understands any change and then the referees, on the Union's behalf, can go back to the districts and the clubs and the players and try to impart this knowledge so that it can be clearly understood. It is therefore very good for a referees' course to take place in parallel with a players' course so that there can be an interchange of ideas; believe me, players and coaches need help in interpretation of the laws and how the game is to develop.

Another important aspect is that interchange of referees must take place in order to improve their standing and understanding, and to try and minimise misinterpretations of the laws. For example, each year there is a meeting established by the Five Nations Committee where referees meet the Five Nations representatives. At that International level, and with only five countries, you would be amazed at the serious differences of interpretation. The idea of that meeting is to eradicate those differences so that the referees in turn can go back to their countries, pass on a general interpretation and so it goes down the line to the other clubs and other societies. Because of the greater number of tours which are taking place now and the growth of independent or neutral referees, it is important that this exchange that I have referred to in the Five Nations takes place on the wider scale so that we can try and cut down the differences of interpretation.

When talking about referees, it always seems funny if one thinks of it in isolation that the referee is the sole judge of fact. Now whether you have any doubts about that, when it comes to the laws of rugby it is literally true, and the referees must receive the support of everybody, not least in the matter of foul play. Such misconduct is appalling for the image of the game and is just intolerable. It's not new, there have been mean twits in the game since time immemorial, and I don't think one can say that rugby is now dirtier than it was twenty or thirty, or even fifty or sixty years ago, but it is under scrutiny. Thousands of people see it all the time, especially at International level, and nowhere in any of your countries can it be tolerated for one man to kick another. It has got no part at all in a strong physical contact game. There is no excuse for referees not being supported in this; they have got only one pair of eyes, they can be unsighted, we all make mistakes and they sometimes do, but still this support has not been as strong as it should. It is something all of us will have to improve immediately because the game is being dragged into disrepute. Unions have to support, clubs have to support, players have to support, captains have to support, coaches have to support, selectors have to support, and when it gets down as far as the clubs, that's five guys sitting in a room on Monday night picking the teams. I give an example of my own club because we

6

have fought hard for a solution and have achieved it. If two members of the Club Committee, either Selection or Executive, see a player of our club kick a man on the field and the referee does not, then that player is automatically brought before the Committee and suspended. It happened twice last season, and it has had a tremendous effect. Foul play is everyone's responsibility.

There is no doubt that the game of rugby football has a right to good administration. The International Board, the top administrative body in the game at the moment, has received criticism in the past, and rightly so. The people who are involved in the game have the machinery for criticism and it must be listened to. But when the International Board does make a pronouncement, it's got no power to enforce it; it is up to the autonomous Unions to do what they think is right within the guidelines or the edict issued. All the more reason why, as I mentioned earlier, we must simplify the laws, not mess with them. You have to have laws, but players do not always understand them. They can't – the laws are too complicated. This is a factor in the current problem of recruiting suitable people for refereeing.

Most players end their career not knowing the laws, and that is probably the first inhibiting factor – they are afraid of being exposed. If a guy wants to go into refereeing he should be encouraged by referees' associations and societies who should say, 'You know the game, you've got something to offer, you can learn the laws and we will teach you.' I am not saying that only ex-players make the best referees (certain International players would probably make appalling ones!), but still it is important.

As I have already said, the game demands and should have proper administration. It is not now a case of dead men's shoes and the good guy who has stayed on long enough and become something. It is all too important now, and no matter what the level – club, province or district, country – everything has to be organised. The people are there if the rugby administrations will go and ask them to do a job and use their expertise for the love of the game. But remember that there are pressures on administrators just as there are pressures on players. These may be more acute in the larger Unions than they are in the smaller ones, but very fortunately the larger Unions at present have excellent professionals. The Welsh Rugby Union have probably led the way in this; they were the first to set up an organisation of development officers and coaches and the men involved, as I say, are excellent, but the game still depends on many thousands of dedicated amateurs and any one of the professionals is the first to agree that his job is futile if he does not have the support of the dedicated amateur. The majority of rugby is being run by dedicated amateurs and this is the way it should be because there is a wealth of talent in rugby administration, but you can kill the horse dead by asking him to do far too much for too long.

For example, the question of the regulations relating to amateurism is constantly under review by the International Board and the related problem of sponsorship is growing in importance. Now there is no doubt that if generous people and commercial firms are prepared to provide rugby football with money it is certainly very acceptable, since the costs of running an amateur game are extraordinarily high. All you have to do is look at the unequalled facilities which the Welsh Rugby Union have worked for and achieved over the years to see what money has to go into rugby, quite apart from helping little clubs to buy grounds with the appalling cost of land these days. But sponsorship must be controlled, and again it is up to the Unions to do this. No commercial firm can run this game. Unions have to be totally responsible, every Union, and must guard against the attraction of all this money coming into the game leading people astray.

Returning, though, to the question of amateurism, I was reading a history of the International Board which was written some years ago and which I would like to quote because in my view it is very pertinent: 'The acid test of our good faith is no longer who is a professional but who is truly an amateur and we dare not forget that this is an amateur game which can be played happily only by amateurs. Once the element of fun, wholehearted enjoyment of the game for its own sake and the friendships which follow, has disappeared from our clubs, the game as we have known it for so many years may well be doomed and with it would disappear a magnificent discipline which strengthens characters.' Now that to my mind is vitally important at this time, even if it may be an over-simplified definition of amateurism to say that a man leaves with no more money in his pocket than he had when he arrived. Such an over-simplification does not deal with the grey areas and heaven knows there are enough of those: gifts not necessarily in cash but possibly in kind, the writing of books and so on. All of these things, as I have mentioned, are under constant review by the International Board, which must pay equal and continuing attention to its own role. It is vitally important as we move into the next era that the Board examines itself, looks critically at its relationship not only to its member Unions but to all of rugby everywhere, lays down certain criteria and aims for the development of the game in every country.

So where do we go from here? Rugby football is a great amateur game for all men wishing to play it, as long as they abide by the laws of the game and the regulations relating to amateurism. There is plenty of room in the game, thank God, for the players who want to play rugby to get fit as well as those who get fit to play rugby. That is its greatness. We cannot jeopardise things for a few who are under pressures at the top. Fitness is important, competitiveness is important, but true sportsmanship has got to be the key.

The game does not belong to Governments. It is not a pawn for politicians nor is it fodder for the less discerning press who would do it down; it belongs to players and it belongs to everyone reading this book. We are only custodians for a short space of time, so we all must resolve to make sure that our particular stewardship is sound, adapting to the present needs as are necessary, but always building on the sound foundation which we have inherited.

I would just like to finish with one quote, a good one when considering our game, from the same history of the International Board to which I referred earlier: 'From boyhood days and our first beginnings down to undiscovered ends, there is nothing worth the wear of winning but the laughter and the love of friends.'

2

A Coaching Philosophy

by J. J. STEWART

'JJ' Stewart is an outstanding coach in all grades of New Zealand rugby and one of the deepest thinkers about the modern game. Although blessed with a sense of humour, he does not suffer fools gladly and speaks forcibly on the game, standing by his beliefs at all times. A brilliant schools and provincial coach first in Taranaki and later at Wanganui, in 1976 he was coach to the New Zealand side in South Africa after being coach on the short tour of Ireland in 1974, where he and manager Noel Stanley proved extremely popular.

The title of the chapter I was invited to contribute to this book was 'A Philosophy of Rugby Coaching'. Now that is a big word in itself. I remember in 1955, when I took an under-21 side to Sri Lanka, giving a team talk to the players, I mentioned 'sophistication' or some such word and Colin Meads said 'JJ, never use a word bigger than "wheatbits" when you are talking to footballers, or they won't know what you are talking about.' So here I am talking about 'philosophy' which is certainly bigger than 'wheatbits'!

Perhaps the first thing is to have a look at just why rugby is such a great game. Above all it is a simple game. Although the skills have to be acquired, they are not difficult to get hold of if they are well taught and if the boys will practise. Contrast it with some of the other games – tennis or athletics for example. There, the individual has to have, as a gift of God or Nature or however you like to think of it, some innate ability that allows him to play that game well. That is why very few indeed get to the top. Rugby is a game that all can play: the fat boy, the thin boy, the not very fast boy, the boy who can't run away from the others in the play-ground. He may have no future in athletics, no eye-hand co-ordination worth talking about, perhaps he can't put a ball to a tennis bat and is a duffer at cricket. But he can play rugby and he can get that intense feeling of belonging to a team that is trying to achieve something. Sure, the ones who are going to the top will have innate ability, but we are not thinking about them all of the time, we are thinking about those hundreds of thousands of kids who play rugby and who want guidance and help and deserve coaching so that they achieve their aspirations in the game.

In Wellington, the capital of my country, the public service have a competition where the police play, as do the Ministry of Agriculture, the Inland Revenue and those sorts of government offices. They only play twenty minutes each way and they are usually clerks and pen-pushers and storemen, who come out all white-legged and knobbly-kneed. Now a couple of years ago the Ministry of Agriculture beat the police in the final of that competition and I met a fellow in a pub a few weeks later who said to me, 'You know, the two greatest games that I have ever seen in my life were the third Test in Auckland in 1937, South Africa v. New Zealand, and the Ministry of Agriculture the day they beat the police.' He was quite sincere and honest about it, too.

But what is this team spirit that, according to what I have just said, young rugby players are going to acquire? For a team to have good team spirit, from a very low age-group right through to International teams, every individual has to realise two things: (a) that other people are depending on his performance, his dedication, his application, his willingness to train and prepare himself for the game, his discipline; (b) that he must rely on fourteen other people, that he can't do it by himself, that it is a team game and that no individual ever succeeded by himself in rugby. This is not a bad thing for young people to realise, however they learn it. If they can learn it in rugby, that's fine, and if it spills over into their lives, their future marriages, their work-place and so on, that's fine, too.

What else has this game of rugby got? Well, a life-time interest. You only have to go to Cardiff Arms Park, Murrayfield, Lansdowne Road, anywhere, to see that the type of person who comes along sticks with his interest in rugby. While it is not a spectacular game, certainly not as spectacular as other games, it

11

has the capacity to produce great drama and not only in top rugby, either.

The next great thing going for rugby is that it is non-professional. Not so long ago I was in Australia and was invited to have a look at Australian Rules, which is a very popular game in the South and West of Australia. It was tremendously, professionally produced, even to dressing-gowns being brought out to the players at quarter-time. It was a great spectacle and it is a spectacular game; it is not unusual for the score to be something like 132 to 110, so there is lots of scoring in it to keep the crowd's interest. But after the game, I said to the people who were hosting me, 'Will the teams now get together?' 'No way,' they said. 'Not on. What are you talking about?' What we have got to hang onto in our amateur approach to the game is the companionship between the teams.

So it's a simple game, it's a game for all types, it's a team game, it creates life-time interest, its got the capacity to produce drama and it's amateur, but we live in difficult times and the game is not immune to them. Rising costs are one problem; I was amazed when somebody told me that the annual lighting bill for some of the grounds in Wales is over £40,000 a year. Whether we like it or not, I'm afraid, rugby is being used as a political tool; we don't want it, we don't seek it, we deplore it and we hate it, but there it is. There is the view, too, that there is too much violence in the game. Whether it is no more violent than it used to be and it is just that there is more of a spotlight on it, I wouldn't know, but the facts are that we are accused of being exponents of a violent game. Over-exposure is a problem: at International level there is unreal pressure on players and administrators (and, I might say, coaches), who are only amateur people.

But the main problem of the game, and the one which I want to deal with at some length, is participation. Are we getting as many young people to come along and play as we used to or are we not? Rugby is a game which is only played by youngsters of 12 or 13 and above; you are damned lucky if you are still in it by your late twenties, and not many people continue to play after thirty, for all sorts of reasons. Since there is nothing, nothing at all, if you haven't got players, the first thing that you have to have is young people who want to play the game. Nobody is going to push them out to play. You can't do it as a military exercise. They have to want to play if you are going to have a game, and you can have coaches, referees' associations, the smoothest-running organisation and the greatest stadia in the world – Cardiff Arms Parks and

Ellis Parks and Murrayfields and Eden Parks – but if you haven't got anybody who wants to go out and play in the middle, then you simply haven't got a game.

So who are the players of today? It is the modern generation, that's who we are talking about. They are the kids upon whom the whole of the future of this game rests and they are sophisticated, they are questioning, they are very knowledgeable, they are confident, and they don't accept bullshit. Now they are a great generation, there can be no argument about that, even if it is an age when the drop-outs and the rat-bags of the generation get all the publicity. But they are very questioning kids and they are not going to stay in a game that they do not enjoy and where they are getting pushed about and bullied and harassed under the name of coaching or whatever and where they don't feel they are making any progress. Significantly, and very significantly from their point of view, there are so many other things available for them today and we are in competition for their attention. They are mobile, they have got money in their pockets and they have got all those other attractions easily enough available to them. Don't forget, either, that this generation has a far easier relationship with the other sex than previous generations had. Now I don't mean that nastily in any way, but boys and girls today are far more interested in doing things together, apart from the old elemental thing, than previously and the things that boys and girls can do together don't include playing rugby. Now time was, and not so long ago either, I dare say, when the only real winter entertainment or recreation available for a lot of young men in places like the Welsh valleys was the rugby club and the rugby game. But today there are all sorts of things available: in New Zealand our kids surf all the year round, and in other countries too. So how are we going to keep them in the game?

I suppose the first question we want to ask is why we want to keep them in the game anyhow? What are we worrying about? These others things are very desirable for them to do and I think anyone genuinely interested in young people is keen to see them do something, for goodness' sake, rather than nothing at all. Don't forget that it is not only sport that is available to them: the drama, arts generally and all sorts of areas reach out to claim their attention and they are thoroughly desirable activities. We can't say to a kid, 'Give up your writing, give up your music, give up your tennis, come and play rugby.' So why do we want them in the game? Well, I think we simply recall the great times and the great fun that we had out of the game and we want them to enjoy the same sort of thing: the companionship, the contest, the thrill of it all. We really want them to enjoy themselves in the manner that we can remember.

Now, how do we keep them in the game? The first thing I am quite sure we have got to produce is a style of game that is fun for them to play and fun for all of them to play, not just the eight forwards up front and the half-back behind them, but the whole lot. If you as a coach think you can produce a pattern of play that is going to win the competition and neglect the aspirations and the fun of half of the team, then you're not serving them because this questioning, sophisticated, knowledgeable generation of kids standing out in the midfield week after week and not doing anything will say, 'To hell with this, this isn't my game at all – all I'm doing is standing here watching those guys have a bit of fun and I'm not having any.' If you have got a team that is having difficulty in employing its backs, the ones who get most of the work are the inside backs, so for goodness' sake change them from week to week and let the kids outside come in and have a go.

So we've got to make more fun for the young players. Then they've got to feel that they are not only enjoying their rugby but progressing as rugby players. It might not be far, it might be a fairly unco-ordinated kid who is certainly not going to play very senior grades at all, but he has got to feel that he is getting somewhere and to this end, I am quite sure that the answer lies in progressive, meaningful, good coaching. That's the key – coaching aimed at the individual's particular progress, his own skills and the team that you are responsible for as a whole unit.

So what is coaching, anyhow? First of all, what it isn't: it isn't press-ups and physical jerks and running round the edge of the field. If they want to do physical jerks and press-ups and run round the edge of the field they can do that in their own time, the coach does not have to supervise that. I have never yet seen a referee give points for anyone doing press-ups or running round the edge of field. So it isn't that. It certainly isn't personal abuse of players, getting a guy out in front of the others and dressing him down about his real or imagined failings. Nor is it dictatorial authority, imposing your ideas on the team without inviting their views on the matter. 'So that's the way this team is going to play and that's the only way it's going to play and anybody who has got any arguments about it can get out of the team' – that's not coaching. Coaching is not coaching smart-Alec, dirty and illegal tactics because they are bound to catch up with the team sooner or later. Thinking of higher grades, coaching is not getting on the booze with the team after the match in the evening and all being good buddy-wuddys together and losing your dignity in the process.

Well, what is it? Coaching in the first instance is coaching individual skills because the whole platform of the game is built on individual skills. What you are usually doing as far as these things are concerned, particularly when the boys are a little older, is constantly correcting faults. Young people, right up to International standard, get into bad habits somewhere, or perhaps they have difficulty with one of the skills. Very few rugby coaches start from absolute scratch: the kids come along, not knowing the laws but knowing the style of the game, they know how you score, they know what you mean by tackle, they know what you mean by pass. I can recall a dreadful experience I had some years ago when a Welshman who was a Minister in the slum area of Adelaide was trying, to his great credit, to get a lot of teenagers off the street by encouraging them to play rugby football. There was no tradition for rugby football in the area whatsoever (it was a Rules area), but he said, 'Rugby's the game' and he got me along to coach. I didn't know where to start – how do you begin to teach rugby to a group of thirty 19-year-olds who have never ever seen the game and never heard about it? Fortunately, that isn't what we have to do, we are usually building on something that is already there or ironing out some problem that has crept in.

Only players can give themselves the skills, but you as the coach have to give guidelines. For example, one of the big problems in the skill area is the question of handedness. Most of us are right-handed, a few of us are left-handed, very, very few indeed are equally capable with both the right and the left hand. What does this mean to rugby? It means that most of the people you coach will kick more easily and more naturally with the right foot, that they will pass the ball to their left more easily than they will to the right because they are pushing it with a strong right hand. They will tackle more easily by driving the right shoulder into an opponent than the left, they will push on the left-hand side of the scrum as a flanker more easily than on the right because they are pushing on a strong right shoulder. A player has to be encouraged to integrate and train the other side of his body, but you are not doing your job as a coach if you say, 'Go and learn to kick with your left foot.' You have got to give him some guidelines. Make him realise that when he is going to kick with his left foot he has to mirror-image what he does with his right foot. If he holds the ball that way to kick with the right foot, then he has got to hold it that way when he is learning to kick with the left foot. Then he has got some guidelines to practise on, and it is up to him to become efficient.

If players have problems with skills, the coach has got to diagnose and come up with the solutions himself. That is a constant part of your job; if you are coaching you can forget about seeing the game because all you see is your own team and their problems and their difficulties. If a player has difficulty with his tackling it is no good saying to him, 'Look, you missed three tackles today. For God's sake tidy up your tackling.' Or 'You let three tries in today because of your poor tackling!' Well, you're pointing out his failings and what you want him to do about it, but what he ought to say then is 'Look, I missed three tackles today, I agree. I'll tell you one thing, coach: I did not sit in the dressing-room before the game and make up my mind that I was going to mess the whole game by missing three tackles deliberately! I didn't want to miss those tackles. If I wanted to miss them I wouldn't be here! You tell me what I'm doing wrong. You tell me why I'm not tackling. You analyse and diagnose my difficulty. I want to tackle, I can't tackle, now you coach me how to tackle!' You're right on the spot, aren't you? You've got to look then and try and decide why he is not tackling. He probably won't say that sort of thing to you, so you've got to go forward and look at him and say, 'He's having trouble tackling and this is why he is having trouble' and then go to him and say, 'I've worked out your problem and we will now start working on its solution.' So watch all the time, and when you see a player improving or trying something that you've encouraged him to have a go at, you've got to notice it. Little things like, 'I saw you have a kick in the match today with your left foot. That's the first time you've ever tried it in a match. Sure, it went over your head and your own full-back caught it, but at least you tried.' Or 'I saw you tackle another man today with your left shoulder, it's coming good.' You have got to notice these things.

Coaching is also about coaching the unit skills. We have got to give our attention to those parts of the game where people come together and operate as a unit: scrum, lineout, ruck, maul, the back line in attack and the back line in defence. They have all got to be coached and practised. Coaching is also paying attention to what I call the mini-units of the game: the two half-backs, the midfield formation, the back three (the two wingers and the full-back), the front five, the loose trio and the half-backs, and that important combination in the modern game of loosies and three-quarters complementing each other and making a mini-unit. What is their job together on the field, how do they mix and operate together, how do they complement each other? Let them practise, give them guidelines.

Sooner or later, coaching is bringing the whole team together and running them as a unit, and that is not an easy job. It is the area where people seem to need most help. What do you actually do with the team when you've got them together? How do you run them as a unit? First of all, there is no such thing as a back coach and a forward coach. If you are going to be a coach you have to learn the techniques and the requirements of the whole team. You have got to become proficient and knowledgeable about scrums and lineouts and mini-units and back lines. It doesn't matter at all what your own playing background was, you have got to re-learn it. You can never do too much with that team, over and over and over again. You can't overdo working with the ball as a team, provided they are doing the right things – and it is your job to make sure that they *are* doing the right things.

Coaching is knowing the laws thoroughly, because you can't cover that important aspect of the game just by inviting a referee along to talk to the team. Little queries about the laws are going to come up at all sorts of times, and you can't just say, 'Right, we'll forget about it all now and we'll have a night halfway through the season when we'll all sit down and discuss the laws and we'll get a referee along.' It doesn't work that way.

You have got to set the team pattern and here is the main point of this chapter: you have got to make your players think, you have got to communicate with them, listen to their ideas and incorporate their ideas into what the team pattern becomes. They are members of a questioning, knowledgeable generation who want to be involved in the decision-making and you, in effect, chair the meeting. Make them think. In New Zealand, and I guess it is pretty much the same world-wide, many rugby players are very good physical specimens from their toe-nails to their eye-balls – it is just from there upwards that they go to pieces! There is only four inches of it, but it is a very important bit! Now we don't exercise it very often. So make them think. Draw your ideas from them. Some years ago I had a provincial team in New Zealand that wasn't doing too badly, and we had a lot of this communication about how they were going to play. At a party later in the year one of the wingers was talking to my wife, and I overheard him say, 'You know, we worked out all the year the pattern we were going to play, and I've just realised that we spent the whole time playing exactly the way that the old bugger wanted us to.' It was one of the proudest moments of my life because they had worked it out but they had come to the conclusion that I had wanted them to come to.

You can do a very great deal of good with a team by sometimes not practising physically but sitting down and having a talk, particularly on cold, wet nights when it is not possible to stop and talk outside because you have to keep the players warm. Forget it – bring the players inside and have a chat about things. I find one of the most interesting and productive ways of getting the team to talk is to make them analyse the tries that were scored against them. Sit them down and say, 'Right, now just after half-time last Saturday our opponents scored a try. Where did it start, how did it happen?' and let them all give you their particular version. You'll find at the start that the versions of how that try was scored are incredible, but the next time a try is scored against them, you can almost hear the brains ticking over as they wait under the posts for the conversion to be taken, while they work out what they are going to say at next week's talk about the matter! So remember, you just chair the meeting.

Probably everybody reading this book has in his head some ideal pattern that he would just love to have a team play, but I don't think even International coaches get the opportunity to spread that pattern out on the field of play. There is always some limitation, something which isn't quite there but is required for that pattern. So you have to work to a pattern that is going to be possible for the players that you've got at your disposal to play. It's no good setting them impossible goals.

You also have to define success, and that too must be realistic. It is silly saying, 'Success for us this year is winning the competition' if you were last the previous year. Success has got to be defined in some more attainable way than that, and the best thing is to set success as doing well, making progress, being a better and more effective team at the end of the season than at the beginning.

You are responsible for running practices if you are coaching, and they must be planned. It it pointless going along to the practice session and then scratching your head and saying, 'Well, I wonder what I'm going to do today.' I put practices into three categories. The first is remedial, where something is obviously wrong: we didn't win as many lineouts last Saturday as we should have done, our scrums weren't very effective, perhaps there were breakdowns in our midfield play. Remedy it by training, talking about it, thinking about it, practising it, getting it right. Second, progressive practices are where we feel we are going right, we've got that far in our team progress and now we can go on and add a bit more. We can do something a bit more imaginative, more interesting, more effective. The third sort of practice is consolidation, where you get to a certain point during the year (usually about a third of the way through the season) and now it's a matter of holding the line, keeping your team interested, not letting them get stale, keeping them going and consolidating the position to which you have progressed.

I don't really know very much about rugby except two things: one, there is more than one way to play it, and secondly, no team ever won because the coach was fit. So you don't have to rip around the bloody field and say, 'Follow me, boys!' You don't have to say, as I heard some fellow say one day, that you would never ask your team to do anything you can't do. If that is the case, you should still be playing.

You are responsible for team organisation and that is just a little thing, but it means a lot. It doesn't take much time, but who is doing what on the field, who exactly is taking the penalty kick, who is kicking for touch? All those sort of things have to be talked about and worked out. Who is covering who from the reserve bench? On one memorable occasion an International team had to have a tremendous discussion when one of their players came off the field before it was decided who went down to replace him. It should all be worked out so that the reserve is sitting there and saying to himself, 'Right, I'm covering him and him and him and him and if any of those fall, I'm on.' That's just organisation, simple straightforward administration of a team.

Don't coach anything that is beyond the laws because sooner or later it'll catch up on you and anyhow it's bad ethics.

Don't coach anything that won't succeed against the best opposition that you are likely to meet. This is often a problem with good school teams or junior teams who carry all before them and begin to think they are great. Really they are just being mis-matched, and one day they strike a team that is as good as them and all that they have been doing doesn't work because there hasn't been anything there anyhow. They have just been running past people who won't tackle them, then suddenly they find someone who will and their whole pattern falls apart. So don't be fooled, and don't let them be fooled. Introduce factors into your pattern that will succeed against the best opposition.

Once you have set your pattern, let the flair of the individual come through. Don't iron it out. If a boy can swerve, encourage him to swerve. If he can side-step, help him to improve it. If he's got a natural change of pace, encourage him to develop it. But don't get hold of a boy and say, 'I'm going to teach you to swerve, to side-step and to change pace' because none of them is like that. You have got to analyse what he might be able to do pretty well and encourage him to do it, but don't cut out flair.

There are other pitfalls to avoid, and one of the commonest is what I call retrospective coaching. This is when you are invited along to a club and given a team to coach, and you say, 'Oh well, I've really been out of the game for some time and haven't had a hell of a lot to do with it. Now let me think – what did our coach use to do when I was playing? Yes, I remember, first he used to make us run round the field ten times. Right – around you go boys,' while you think what he did next! Even if it was a very good coach you had, times have changed and that type of coaching will not fit the modern game. So don't remember how you were coached and think that it will do now. It won't.

The next pitfall is a failure to adjust to this constantly changing and evolving game. It is not only the result of law-changes, although they often alter the whole face of the game, but the game's pattern, its ideas. We nourish each other internationally, so if a technique develops in Wales, say, it is copied by the rest of us, and vice versa. Any coach has got to watch all the time what is happening, learn from anybody, never shut his eyes or ears to any suggestion that is made to him at all. For example, I have always been very interested in the French flair, the French pattern and the French style. It is hard to find out what they do because I was taught French very carefully in my country, and when I speak to the French team they can't understand me! It's very difficult to get anything out of a country that can't speak its own tongue! But I was watching them play one day and it was a matter of trying to work out step by step exactly what they were doing. I went into the toilet at half-time and an old fellow came in, he lined up alongside me and started to get his arrangement out. He was having a little bit of trouble and I felt a sort of wetness down in my boot but he said, 'You know, these French are cunning buggers! We all stand back in a staircase formation on attack and then we give it away because we come up flat as soon as we get the ball. They line out and they stay in it as they

20

attack.' And I looked at him and I said, 'Well, that's so bloody right! That's dead right! If you can teach me something else you can come round and piss on the other boot!!' It was a simple little thing that I hadn't been able to see, but this old rooster, he had seen it and I was very grateful to learn from him.

Another pitfall is taking credit for yourself for things that don't really happen. You say, 'Right, boys. Now we are going out there today and we are going to do a, b, c and d,' and neither a nor b nor c nor d comes up, but you win because the goal-kicker has a good day and kicks four penalties. As the team comes off, you say, 'There you are, fellas – didn't I tell you that would work?' That is very easy to do because we have to live with the fact that if a team wins it is a damned good team, and if it gets beaten it needs a new coach. So we never win.

Don't get into the pitfall that was hinted at by Ronnie Dawson in his Introduction of running the game from the sidelines. It is not your game, it is their game. You've got duties and responsibilities and functions in the matter, but it is their game. I always say to a team that whatever the captain decides on the day, even if it ends in disaster, has my full support and I will stand behind him. Let them play it. They are at the actual work-face, we are not.

Don't regard coaching as mere motivation. I know an All Black in New Zealand who was in the position of having to coach his own club side, and he said to me, 'Look, they don't come to training, they turn up twenty minutes before the game and start cleaning their boots, they've been out on the booze Friday night, they're not concerned at all really. Then they sit down and expect me to give them a talk that is going to change them from bloody rubbish into giants in five minutes, and if they don't win the game they come in and say that I didn't motivate them properly.' Some people have the ability to give a highly motivating talk to players before a game; if you can do it, good. If you can't, don't try to do it. Don't try and copy other people. You have got to be your own man in this game and develop your own style and your own technique. Provided it is soundly based it will be alright. Get your team together, particularly a more senior team, and have a talk to them before the game, but if you're not good at the high-pressure stuff, just talk about the pattern, quieten them, bring their minds together. This is what we are doing, this is what we have decided we are going to do, this is our approach, this is what our opponents are, this is how good they are, this is our previous experience of them. Reserves, do you know who you are

21

covering, are you quite sure of all the organisation points? I remember going down to the South Island of New Zealand once and hearing the coach giving a tremendous harangue to a team who were going to play my fellows at the time, and I went back and I said, 'Goodness me, I don't know what's going to happen today but somebody's getting them stirred up in there like the bloody Battle of Waterloo is coming up!' Anyhow, after the game I said to a very experienced player on the other team, 'How does a bloke like you with your experience react to that sort of thing?' He replied, 'Well, I find if you stare at the floor it's always thought that you are concentrating!'

Because this chapter is about philosophy and ethics is a branch of philosophy, we had better have a look at coaching ethics. There is no doubt in my mind that the coach is responsible for his team's attitude to the game. It is not the referees' responsibility to clean up the game of rugby on their own. Referees have been asked to do it and I support the International Board and all the Unions in asking the same thing, but the referees shouldn't be put in that position. A referee is a person who gives up his afternoon so that thirty young men can have their game of rugby, and it is the coaches who should impose an attitude towards the game that does not include irresponsible, dirty, unfair or foul play.

Another ethical point: don't rip up a player nastily in front of his team-mates. If you have got something critical to say about his attitude, take him away by himself, put your big finger in his chest, say what you like, but it is only a game, he doesn't deserve to be embarrassed in front of his team-mates. Occasionally saying something to him in front of his team-mates could be on, but not an abusive tirade.

Don't encourage players to hide their failings behind the referee. It is a very easy habit for teams to get into; they come off the field and say that the referee was so and so, and so and so. Let them have a good bitch for five minutes, then shut them up. A good way is to say quietly, 'Do any of you fellows really think that the referee made more mistakes today than you did?' That usually finishes that bit.

I don't think, ethically, that coaches can get drunk. Your dignity is important, so get drunk away from the team, and don't go chasing the waitresses in the hotels and that sort of thing. You are in charge of the players on and off the field. Rugby isn't well served by those end-of-season trips that are nothing more or less than drunken, sexual orgies. The game is too precious for such goings-on to be masqueraded under its name and don't forget that in that sort of thing the coach sets the tone. The paradox is that if teams go away to play and they are concentrating on the rugby, they have a damned good time. If they are using rugby as the opportunity to go away and misbehave, then they don't have such a good time.

If a team's got a manager, whatever level it is, you must support him. If he says the bus is leaving at such and such a time, you ensure that the team reacts to it. People have often asked me what is the true role of manager and assistant manager or coach on an international tour. I recall being in Perth with the All Blacks in 1974 and we agreed to play on a Sunday to avoid a clash with the Australian Rules which are so popular and were being played on the Saturday. So the local Union wanted to entertain us on the Saturday and they said, 'Some of you can go to the races and some of you can go to the Rules.' The manager and I agreed that one of us would go to the races and one would go to the Rules. He asked me which I would like to go to and I said, 'Thanks very much, Les, I'd like to go to the races.' He replied, 'Tough luck, you're going to the Rules!' So that's the difference!

Never forget that as a coach you are in charge of young people, and that's an awesome responsibility. You, whether you like it or not, become part of their growing up, and an important part of it, because if they are interested in the game it sort of fills their lives. Your own standards must be high because they are going to accept your standards – your standards and attitudes to the game and to normal accepted morality. Be authoritative but not heavy-handed and always keep slightly at a distance, even at International level. If you pass through Singapore with an International team and everybody scoots down to have a look at Boogy Street, in my book the coach doesn't go, he just keeps that little bit removed.

The basic philosophical question that this chapter has not yet asked is why are we in it anyhow? Coaches spend time, they lose money. Why? A couple of years ago, a Minister of Religion giving the morning talk on the radio said that there is a vast generation gap between the youth of today and the older generation, and he claimed that the reason is that the older generation have opted out of giving care, attention and interest to the modern generation. If I'd known who he was I'd have rung him up and told him to come and have a look at the rugby scene, at people who are giving up time to referee, to administer and to coach, taking responsibility for those kids and part of their growing up. Then let's see if he's got anything to say about the generation gap.

Philosophy down the ages has concerned itself with the question of love – not physical love, but that interwoven mattress of threads of affection that make up human relationships. In coaching there must be two basic loves. First, a love of the game, and for no reason – not because it's a way of life, not because it's a religion, not because it's any of those silly things claimed for it at all, just because it's rugby and we love the game for itself. Secondly, the love of the players; you've got to love the young men and the boys who play the game and be prepared to give time and attention and interest to them. If you've got that sort of attitude, everything else fits in. You won't let them down and you'll go on trying to develop as a better coach.

But it's a silly old game really, isn't it? If a man from Mars came down and saw it he would wonder what was happening. People fall over in a heap, somebody blows a whistle, they get up and they're formed into two organised teams – the man from Mars wouldn't understand it, but there it is. This silly old bumbling, wonderful, magnificent game of rugby can give growing kids so much; not only can it offer them recreation and fun and the opportunity to play, but it can teach them team spirit, it can teach them the experience of victory and the joy that goes with it, it can teach them to bite on the bullet hard when they've been beaten, and it can be part of their growing up and developing. They're the future, they're the heirs to the ages, and that is really what it's all about.

3

Refereeing – An Alternative Philosophy

by CORRIS THOMAS

As well as Home Internationals, Corris Thomas has refereed the national teams of New Zealand (three times), Australia, Argentina, Canada, USA, Tonga, several 'B' Internationals, schools and youth Internationals, the Barbarians and the Welsh Cup Final. He has been to the USA on three occasions in order to referee, lecture and hold seminars.

This chapter presents a personal view of the relationship between the referee, the laws of rugby and the game itself, and suggests that there is one definitive, overall philosophy of refereeing that is more appropriate than any other to the betterment of the game.

Five requirements must form the first cornerstone of any refereeing philosophy. Every referee should be able to satisfy all these requirements and every player is entitled to expect them from a referee every time that referee runs onto a pitch. He must be:

1 Up with play
2 Correct in law
3 Consistent
4 Decisive
5 Cool.

No doubt nearly all referees – and certainly those who referee seriously – will claim to possess all these attributes but, over the last few years especially, it would appear that these qualities are just not enough in view of the considerable criticism of the standard of refereeing that has come from all corners of the rugby world. There has been expressed in private, and in public through the Press, concern as to differences in interpretation, differences in approach and inconsistencies between one referee and another. As referees we must ask ourselves whether such criticisms have an element of truth, and if so, what mistakes are being made? Why they are being made and what can be done to eliminate them?

Even allowing for ill-informed opinion, this chapter suggests that the fault lies firmly with the referees in that they have been guilty of being too inward-looking, too obsessed purely with the law-book, concentrating far too much on legal trivialities and technicalities and not standing back and asking themselves what the game requires and what contribution the laws and referees can make to the game. Plato defined the philosopher as 'one who apprehends the essence or reality of things in opposition to the man who dwells in appearances and the shows of sense'. What referees must do is look for the essence and reality of things by a return to basics and to the question 'where does our first responsibility lie?' The answer to this question is that each referee's responsibility must be to the players and to them alone. It is not to the spectators or to other referees or to the Press, but to the players who train and are coached, and for whom the laws were designed and the game created.

This being the case, the initial requirement of a referee is to obtain the players' confidence. If this can be done, then refereeing becomes so much easier and better. It means that the referee must give the impression from the start that he is not out to get at players, that he is not there to show how well he knows the laws, but he is there to help them play the game in the way they have been coached, within the broad framework of the laws.

On a practical level, it helps to obtain the players' confidence if the referee explains his decisions. It cannot be overstressed that every player is entitled to know why the referee has blown his whistle. The game is so fluid, there are so many laws that can be broken, both intentionally and unintentionally, that the players should expect to be told precisely the reason why the whistle has been blown. For example, the referee should tell the front row specifically if the scrum-half has been penalised; they will have had their heads in the scrummage, so will not have known what has gone on behind them and may well believe that they have incurred the penalty themselves. Referees should talk to the players and explain to them what they are trying to do. This doesn't mean a running commentary on the game any more than it means carrying on conversations with players. It means the referee making the players aware of what he is trying to do, which is to organise a platform upon which the game can be played.

As well as this platform, a game also needs rhythm since it is extremely difficult to play rugby in an atmosphere of stop/go/stop/go. The chances are that the fewer times the whistle is blown and the fewer times that play stops, the better the game of rugby which will be played. When the referee runs onto the pitch he must run on with the conviction that his job is to control the game as a whole rather than to exercise command by dealing with a multitude of separate incidents in their own right. He is there not to search for illegalities but to attempt to produce an atmosphere conducive to the playing of good football by means of fair play.

The second cornerstone of the philosophy set out in this chapter is that there are four specific areas of law that need to be refereed strictly for the benefit of the game. These are as follows:

1 Foul play, misconduct and obstruction, because they are destructive, dangerous, negative and unfair.
2 Collapsing scrums, also because they are destructive, dangerous, negative and unfair.
3 Deliberately infringing Laws 18 and 19, that is the tackle law, and the law relating to players lying on the ground with or near the ball. Referees *must* punish those players whose intention it is to kill the ball whether under Laws 18 or 19 or at rucks. Such play is negative, destructive and unfair, and it is destroying a facet of the game where the greatest opportunities for constructive rugby become available.
4 Backs encroaching within ten metres at the lineout. Again, this is a negative move which is denying the other side a substantial area of ground in which to play constructive rugby.

The next step is to consider the nature of the laws themselves, to try to get them into proper focus, and it is this which is the fundamental purpose of this chapter. Referees must go back to the beginning and ask themselves the questions, 'Why are laws necessary? Why are laws created?' The answer is that the laws of rugby, just like the law of the land, exist so that human behaviour can be organised in such a way as to conform to a civilised pattern, and in order to give both teams an equal chance of scoring points.

Laws should not be seen as an end in themselves, so even though they may appear to be mandatory, penalties cannot be intended to apply on every single occasion a law is broken. To take a non-rugby example, a car is parked on a double yellow line in the middle of Cardiff at 2 am on a Sunday morning: the law has been broken but the chances are that the driver will incur no penalty. Compare that with parking the car in the same spot at 9 o'clock on a Monday morning: without any doubt the driver will be booked. In each case there has been an infringement of the law but in one case no penalty has been given. At 9 o'clock on the Monday morning no more laws were broken and yet a penalty was incurred. What is the justification for penalising one and not the other? It is a maxim that operates within our legal system – 'de minimis non curat lex', which means 'the law ignores trivialities'. If it didn't, life would become extremely difficult, if not impossible. It has to be emphasised that it is *not* a question of opting out of the laws, it is a question of applying the maxim which is an underlying principle of our legal system. Also it does *not* imply the omitting of any laws – all laws are enforced, but only when the circumstances for which those laws were created actually happen.

The criticism that has been made of referees is to a large extent the result of referees not applying this legal maxim to the laws of rugby. Referees have been taking Law 6(a)(3) too literally: 'the referee shall keep the time and the score and he must in every match apply fairly the laws of the game without any variation or omission'. What I am suggesting is nothing more than that the referee administers the laws of rugby in exactly the same way as the laws of the land are administered. On a practical level, what does this mean? It means that penalties should be given not simply because a law has been broken but only where there has been, in addition, an effect from the breaking of the law; after all, that is why the law was created in the first place.

For example, imagine a scrummage near the goal line and near the touch line. The attacking side puts in the ball which comes out through channel 3. The players have planned a blind-side move. However, the defending side's wing, some fifty yards away on the open side, wanders two or three yards off-side. Meanwhile, the attacking scrum-half passes to his blind-side winger who is bundled into touch. In these circumstances the defending open-side winger should not be penalised because there has been no effect whatsoever through his breaking the law. He has neither gained his side an advantage nor prevented the opposition from getting an advantage. He is quite simply out of the game. If, on the other hand, an open-side back movement had developed, then he might well have had an effect on play and of course he would have been penalised.

Another example, from a lineout. The ball is thrown to the back man. Very often in these circumstances the front man in the lineout automatically steps over the line of touch in order to see where the ball has gone. He is off-side and has broken the law. But the ball is tapped down by the back-marker to his scrum-half who is running in-field, and the ball is passed out to the three-quarters. Again, the referee need not penalise the front man in the lineout because he is out of the game. Conversely, however, if that front man in the lineout crossed the line when the ball was thrown to no. 2 or no. 3 in the line, then the chances are that he will have had an effect on the lineout either by gaining an advantage for his own side or by preventing his opponents from obtaining an advantage. In that case, although no more laws have been broken, there may well be a case for penalising him.

A third example is taken from an International match. A scrum took place on the halfway line. A flanker, momentarily unbound, took a half-step forward and then, realising the ball was not coming out of the opponents' scrum, re-bound. No opposition player was aware that he had re-bound in such a fashion; probably the only person near the scrummage who saw it was the referee. Yet he penalised the flanker and the attacking side kicked a penalty goal, although the legal infraction had had no effect on the game whatsoever. The flanker had neither gained an advantage nor prevented an advantage to the opposing side. Indeed, if the scrum had been frozen at that particular point, it is highly likely that the referee would have found that maybe one, two or even more members of the front row had slipped their binding or had gone down too low.

What you have to do, then, before awarding a penalty is to ask the questions, 'Why is the penalty to be given?' and 'Why is it necessary?' Ask yourself these questions each time the law is broken. It is not an easy thing to do: it requires an understanding of the game, a feel for the game and an appreciation of the atmosphere of the match. It also requires confidence, coolness and, if refereeing in Wales, a deaf ear to the exhortations for penalties from the spectators! It is a very heavy responsibility on a referee, but if he seeks to improve himself then it is something that he must take upon himself. Referees should remember that the object of the game as set out in the law-book is not 'to score the most points and never break the laws', but to win 'through *fair play* according to the laws' (my italics). What referees must ensure is that a side does not win through unfair play, remembering always that simply breaking a law does not of itself constitute unfair play.

What we really come down to are penalties, which, if the causes of discontent are analysed, are probably at the root of the problems that have been highlighted over the past few years. This can be illustrated from an article that was written in the *Sunday Times* newspaper some time ago, the relevant section of which is as follows:

'The word is out. Referees are blowing their whistles more often this season than they used to. It has nothing to do with violent play either. Players have grumbled about unsympathetic refereeing for years – it is much a part of rugby fabric as drinking and dirty songs. Now, though, it is not only the players that are commenting about it. Former international referee Larry Lamb and Hermas Evans, a member of the WRU Referees' Committee, have also noticed. So has Mick Titcomb, a former international referee. "I think sometimes referees are too preoccupied with the technicalities of the game instead of encouraging the players to play the game," says Titcomb.

'The invalidity of this approach was pointed out in Alan Bean's pamphlet, *The Art of Refereeing*, published by the RFU in 1950. "Refereeing", he wrote, "is neither a science nor yet the job of a lawyer, still less that of a policeman." Yet the cliché image of a referee behaving like a whistle-happy traffic policeman is one that many players use as they seek to explain the resentment. What they want is the sort of sympathy that manifests itself in the quiet word at the right time.'

This concern was recognised by rugby administrators and was reflected in the exercise that was carried out by them a few years ago where, on a world-wide basis, an analysis was made of the numbers of penalties that were given in a random selection of matches and also the reason for those penalties. The results make fascinating reading and are summarised in Tables 1, 2 and 3.

The introduction of the differential penalty has made but a small dent in the problem represented by the disappointing statistics in Table 1; it does not and cannot get to its root. If the nature of the game is not to change through constant and fundamental law-changes, the only solution lies in referees re-

Table 1

	Wales	All countries
Total matches	66	442
Total penalties	1604	9689
Total penalties kicked	141	962
Penalties per match	24	22
Penalties kicked per match	2.3	2.2
% of penalties kicked	9.6	10.1
Matches where result affected by penalties:		
Number	16	87
As a % of all matches	24	20

thinking their approach to the game and to the laws in the way that I have already suggested.

From Table 2 it is interesting to observe that half of all penalties are given for scrummage and lineout offences, areas of the game whose purpose is simply to re-start proceedings, and that even though the lineout is generally thought to be the game's real problem area, scrummage offences exceed lineout offences by 50%. The reason lies in Table 3, which gives the reasons for the award of each penalty. It makes interesting and disturbing reading. An analysis of the penalties given for scrummage offences shows that over half were given for foot up or not in straight. In Wales such penalties amounted to 241, yet the total number of penalties given for collapsing, lowering and not binding was only 51. Clearly such an imbalance is wrong, especially since collapsed scrums have become an increasing blot on the game over the last few years. Even though foot up and crooked

Table 2

Incidence of penalties	
Scrum	30%
Lineout	20%
Ruck	15%
Maul	10%
	75%
General play	25%
	100%

Table 3

	Wales		All countries	
	Number of penalties	*% of total*	*Number of penalties*	*% of total*
Scrum: foot up	97	6.0	588	6.1
not in straight	144	9.0	994	10.3
collapsing	4	0.2	43	0.4
lowering	30	1.9	100	1.0
not binding	17	1.1	85	0.9
handling ball	18	1.1	145	1.5
returning ball	13	0.8	50	0.5
off-side	141	8.8	949	9.8
Lineout: off-side	164	10.2	894	9.2
general	175	10.9	955	9.8
Maul: off-side	124	7.7	714	7.4
general	45	2.8	212	2.2
Ruck: off-side	116	7.2	714	7.4
general	84	5.2	454	4.7
Off-side in general play	145	9.0	1044	10.8
Lying on the ball	37	2.3	248	2.6
Not playing ball	37	2.3	321	3.3
Intentional knock-on	14	0.9	57	0.6
Misconduct/obstruction	161	10.0	899	9.3
Other	38	2.4	233	2.3
Total	1604		9689	

feeds now merit only free kicks, the statistics support my major premise that the referees at the time of this survey were over-obsessed with technicalities; I have seen nothing in recent years which persuades me fundamentally to change this view.

The truth is probably that penalties for foot up and not in straight were easy penalties to give. What referees should have been doing, however, and should do in the future, is to eliminate the need to give such penalties. For example, if at every scrum the referee simply tells the scrum-half to put the ball down the middle quickly, then more often than not the players will take note of the referee and will play according to his standards. There is no need to give penalty after penalty in order to make his requirements known. Again, if a player does stray off-side, as long as he has no effect on the game, the referee can make known to him that he has seen the offence. It is likely that the player will take greater care in the future.

If referees administer the laws in the circumstances in which they were meant to apply, games will be more fluid, more open and less dominated by unnecessary penalties and whistling. More points will be scored and more tries will result, so that the try will assume the importance it deserves.

4

Violence in Rugby

by AIR VICE-MARSHAL
   G. C. ('LARRY') LAMB

One of the leading international referees since the war, Larry Lamb still devotes a great deal of time to rugby matters and can be considered a student of many sports. The rugby laws and the conduct of referees interest him greatly and he believes that rugby can be readily enjoyed with an equal amount of self-discipline and respect for officials and fellow players. He had control of fourteen International matches and has lectured in most of the rugby countries in the world game.

When some years ago the Roman Catholic Primate of All Ireland was invited to give his views on sin he replied simply, 'I'm agin' it.' Almost anyone in the rugby game, invited to give his views on violence in sport, would reply equally sincerely, 'I'm agin' it.' But today's attitudes on this burning topic can be no less ambivalent than were those of that self-same Irish priest when a few days later he was taking confessional and amongst those seeking absolution of their various sins was a prop forward from a Southern Irish and hence predominantly Catholic club. 'Father,' said the prop, 'on Saturday I fouled several opponents quite viciously.'

'Disgusting, my son. What with?'

'Well, Father, I butted the opposing hooker and split his eyebrow open.'

'Shameful! Anything else?'

'Well, I kicked a player in his kidneys when he was lying on the ground.'

'Mother of Mercy! A disgrace to the game you are, my son. What else?'

'Well, I thumped a no. 8 in the lineout, Father, and I knocked him out cold.'

'Well, who were these poor souls, then?'

'Oh, they were a crowd of Ulster Protestants down here on their Easter tour.'

'Well, Lord,' said the priest, 'I guess boys will be boys!'

But before any player, selector, coach, administrator or referee dismisses that story as a light-hearted piece of trivia, he should ask himself whether his attitudes to violence in the game today are not as ambivalent as were those of that mythical Irish priest. For as the newspapers make all too clear, violence on the field and on the terraces is now to be ranked with drug-taking as one of the major sporting evils. It would be easy for me to claim that I have an instant solution, but the history of rugby football is full of instant panaceas that went seriously wrong, so we have to be very chary about how we tackle this problem; it is a deep-seated and complex malaise and the cure must not be worse than the disease.

Law and order, which really means the effective enforcement of the rules by which any society lives, was an electoral issue in Britain at the last election, but unhappily it has for some years now been commonplace for mob violence to seek to overthrow authority to enforce the will of a minority. Even Ministers of the Crown in the last Socialist Government publicly insulted Her Majesty's Judges, joined controversial picket lines and lent their authority to a gradual erosion of respect for our legal system. They overlooked, but we in rugby must never overlook, the fact that the laws of sport and the laws of the land are based on the same principle: namely that the law stands supreme. The PLO, the Red Brigade, the IRA, flying pickets, all of these, in principle at least, are allied to such strange bedfellows as the 1974 British Lions and their infamous '99' call which when literally translated was nothing more sophisticated than an invitation to hit the nearest Springbok in sight, and to the morons who made and presumably sold the pathetic little 'Paul Ringer is Innocent' lapel badge after the 1980 England v. Wales game at Twickenham. It is this sort of evidence which should make us all examine our consciences as we consider our attitudes to violence on the field of play.

In 1955 the President of the Rugby Football Union, the late Sir William, then Mr, Ramsay, wrote in a foreword to O. L. Owen's history of the Union, 'Rugby Football is for the ordinary player and intentionally has not been developed too much to prevent him from enjoyment on that one afternoon of the week which can be spared for the purpose.' In 1967, just over a decade later, in the first of its coaching pamphlets, the same Rugby Football Union was moved to state that 'our attitudes and our standards have failed to give us rugby football of a quality that we know could and should be played. They have prevented us reaching performance levels that others have shown themselves capable of achieving.' This was a major turnabout in the game's philosophy, and the will to win, almost at any price, became firmly implanted at all levels of the game. To many in these islands, the reflected glory from victories in the early 1970s over the hitherto invincible All Blacks and Springboks was in itself justification for this change of approach. At the same time there was a marked improvement in playing skills which was not matched by corresponding improvements in refereeing recruitment, training, assessment, selection or performance.

At this point it is perhaps not irrelevant to refer to the objective of rugby union football as laid down by the International Board in their preamble to the laws of the game which states that 'two teams of fifteen players each, observing fair play and a sporting spirit, should by carrying, passing and kicking the ball score as many points as possible. The team scoring the greater number of points to be the winner of the match.' A. A. Thomson, in his book *Rugger My Pleasure*, said much the same thing but in different words: 'It's a game of grace and skill, but it's a game of such vigour that for the sake of the Queen's peace, for very life's sake, it has to be a game of sportmanship and good temper. If it is not, it will not survive as a game. It becomes impossible without law and order.' Let me quote further from Edward Grayson's splendid book, *Sport and the Law*: 'There is no doubt where the law stands and has stood for a century. From 1878 to the present day, the British Courts have sustained the same principles of reckless and deliberate violent action. . . . Tackle fairly and there is no problem, tackle foully but accidentally and there will be no legal liability, but tackle foully or hit below the belt with deliberation and/or recklessness and there is no doubt what the consequences would and should be: a criminal prosecution and a claim for damages.' That day has already arrived.

That there has been violence in sport in the past few can deny. But now it is a field of activity in which millions participate and on occasions hundreds of millions observe. Success in this field is often given a political dimension so that the world's peoples find in the achievements of their sportsmen a meaning that often transcends the sport itself. It is true that the significance of these achievements is transitory, but of one thing we can be certain: through the activities of the media and of commercial sponsors each situation will be exploited to the full and as a result the overall popularity of sport is unlikely to diminish. It is in this modern framework of opportunity and achievement that we must view the problem of violence in our game.

Nor should we ever forget that sport is important principally because it forms values and attitudes. It is a sort of education, one which enables an individual to discipline his actions and increase his efficiency. It can be a source of health and a preparation for manhood, as well as merely escapism or a relief from monotony. It can bring its return in terms of self-awareness, self-discipline and the capacity to work with others, while at representative level it can contribute to the community-building process and can foster great national pride. Should we not all be striving to translate these virtues through sport into the very fabric of our everyday life? The tragedy of violence in sport arises because we seem to have put the cart before the horse and are translating the characteristics of violence, now part and parcel of our daily life, into our sport.

It is, of course, often claimed that rugby football epitomises the virtues that I have just described as well as any type of sport. It might seem sacrilegious even to question whether its ethos is changing, but with my background I am only too well aware that the much-maligned word 'discipline' and the thing itself are as out of fashion as are hansom cabs. The discipline we need most of all in rugby football is self-discipline, a man's control of his own actions and his own attitudes of mind. J. B. Priestley wrote recently, 'So many people today seem to imagine that they have been freed from harsh conditions to do whatever they please. They have left behind the challenging rocks of discipline by circumstance, yet they cannot reach the shining plateau of self-discipline.' We in rugby cannot escape this daftness which imagines our society is gaily floating along to a happier future when in fact we know it is half-sinking.

Strong statistical evidence to support this in the rugby scene is provided by the steady increase in the number of sendings-off each season. What are the implications and where lies the solution? Clearly the restoration of self-discipline, both by the players themselves and by those who select and coach them, is essential. Equally, but perhaps even more important, we need men of quality and character to control this game of physical contact, and the type of control exercised over games by referees must change in emphasis as violence continues to increase. It now needs to be exercised more on the individual player than on the game overall; there is a greater need for players to be taught self-control rather than our automatically assuming that they possess it. At the same time we must recognise that the pressures on both teams and individuals are more intense, the stakes and the rewards are higher, demands are now differently and more finely balanced between those of the game itself, the individual players, the spectators and the media. Firmness, fairness and consistency are the key attributes of the successful referee – better to be the respected bastard than the despised weakling – but the roles of the captain and the coach in controlling the behaviour of individual players now requires re-emphasis.

What are the other possible remedies? An oppressive attitude at school or in the junior club could discourage the desirable development of the pupil and lead him to drop out from active play, but license or slackness on the part of officials at school or junior games is bad. It is at this stage that discipline and the ethos of the game must be taught and inculcated effectively. It is essential to get the message across at the lower levels and then maintain it, but equally, courage on the part of administrators to impose appropriate and tougher penalties when they are justified is a prerequisite for success. So is a need for effective administrative and disciplinary procedure. Moreover, we need adequate recruitment of referees, induction training to acquire experience, mental and physical alertness, and regular monitoring of performance by assessors or adjudicators who are both guardians of standards and mentors of the man with the whistle.

The approach of the media is also important and we must somehow bring them to condemn rather than in a sense condone violence by the way they treat it. The principal conclusion of the Rugby Union's Conference for Overseas Unions at Bisham Abbey some years ago was not a request for money, for representation on the International Board, for more visits from foreign International teams, for subsidised publications or playing gear. This is what they said: 'The overriding sense of this Congress is that the Rugby Football Union should take up with the International Board the necessity for positive action in order to reduce the incidence of violence in all matches played, but more particularly in those matches which are publicised to the world rugby community through the medium of television, films, radio and the Press. The desire of the Congress is that all games played under the jurisdiction of the International Board should be examples of the true spirit of the ethos of the game.'

The 'positive action' asked for is still lacking, for although the International Board has emphasised clearly the duty of member Unions to ensure that the game at every level is conducted in accordance with disciplined and sporting behaviour, there is evidence that duty is being shirked. 'Boys will be boys' is an unacceptable response when bones can be broken and blood spilt for no other reason than to win a game of football. But the Board itself, by delegating authority, cannot shirk the responsibility for the violence in the game. All too frequently laws have been changed without any realisation of their impact and their contribution to the problem. I would like to see every major law-change made experimental for a minimum of two years before being finally incorporated in the laws as a permanent measure. I would also like to see all such proposals put through a sort of clearing house comprised of top-class referees, players and coaches before even being submitted to the International Board itself. This implies no diminution of the Board's authority nor disrespect for its status, rather the reverse; there has been nothing edifying about the way in which so many recent law-changes have had to be either rescinded or further explained by directives. Such a consultative body would free the Board from the necessary detail of devilling and debating which is involved when they formulate the compromise laws which so often represent the midway positions between the many individual proposals put up by member Unions. Such a body would also be ideally suited to examine the flashpoints of the game, those areas which give rise to frayed tempers and subsequent violence.

This naturally leads on to the role of coaches in this vexed problem. For example, the art of rucking, as practised in particular by New Zealand, is clearly here to stay. Now the average All Black forward would tell you that the reason why anyone gets hurt in a ruck is because they persist in lying on the ball, and there is perhaps a message here for us British referees in particular. Nevertheless, jumping on top of players in a ruck, as is practised nowadays, is and always has been illegal, and I am amazed at the way some coaches teach it and some referees allow it to go on. The coach, of course, is in a difficult position because he knows what he wants – the ball – and he would argue that it is up to the referee to apply Law 19 in a way which will ensure that the players who are there at the point of breakdown first eventually get the ball. But any coach who coaches such an illegality as climbing in on a ruck in order to achieve this end is not only ignoring the object of the game and the laws themselves, but is as guilty at least by association as is the player who commits the violence on the field. The moral as well as the practical responsibility of today's coaches to preserve the ethos of the game is as great as that of any of the players they control.

Finally, I must bite on the bullet and try to answer the question, what can or should the referee do about violence? I have already touched on certain facts which he must face. First, we live in an age and in a society where dissent and violence are becoming increasingly accepted as a means of asserting a point of view or of propagating a cause. Second, this fact has spilled over into sport because of the pressures now placed on players to win which in turn leads to an ambivalent attitude on the part of selectors, coaches and administrators towards the methods used to win. Third, the trend is unlikely to be halted, at least in the short term. Fourth, many top-class referees have little or no experience and have been given little or no guidance or training in the handling of this relatively new phenomenon. Fifth, at the higher levels, the name of the game is winning. Any top referee who fails to hoist in that absolutely fundamental point is deluding himself and living in 'cloud-cuckoo land'. He must know and understand exactly how the teams that operate at this level set about their business of winning and which aspects of that business could explode into violence.

Very few of the top referees have ever played the game at International level, and even the few who have can very quickly get out of date. To fill this gap in the knowledge of our top-class referees, a couple of years ago the Rugby Union asked some leading coaches to teach our top referees actually how to ruck and maul and scrummage and play the lineout. The object was not to teach them actually to do it as an end in itself, but rather to ensure that they could more readily understand, for example, just what the physical pressures are on props or hookers in a scrum, or what the opportunities are for disruption in a lineout. Thus they could more readily appreciate the lengths to which some players will go either to exert or to avoid these pressures and to enable them, of course, to withstand the reactions of their opponents.

If you think I am exaggerating the importance of understanding modern techniques, think of the players who have been coached to play within the laws and whose skills are being negated. Given the current attitudes within society, is it any wonder that they become disenchanted with the absence of any constraints and press to be allowed to take the law into their own hands? The days are gone when the players simply got on with their thing while the referees did the same.

In one's early days as a referee one is adjured to take onto the field no preconceived ideas about players or teams. As an idealistic principle it is incontrovertible, but as a guide to events in top-level rugby it is positively misleading. Forwarned is fore-armed.

My last point concerns the occasion itself. Every top-class match, particularly an International match, is important in its own right. It will always be important to the participants: a win may be a launching pad to distinction, failure and a loss may mean oblivion. It will make and mar the day for tens, maybe hundreds, of thousands of spectators. So do not ever go onto the field at the top level believing it's only a game – it isn't really. If, as a result, your failings lead to violence, then the image of this great game is tarnished just a little bit further. All referees at that level must be prepared to concentrate and work as they've never concentrated or worked before, not just for some of the time but for eighty minutes. Their work-rate must place them amongst the Trojans of the refereeing world, for the junior club game norm will not be enough. It will call for physical and mental efforts that will drain you. Every lineout, every scrummage must be observed in all its facets with single-mindedness. Every ball must be chased wherever it goes. Your head must be rolling to the left and to the right. You have to be mindful of but not swayed by the players' or the crowd's reaction. A violent movement or an anguished howl in the scrum may be the first clue to an illegality or a violent act, and the crowd's roar may alert you to an event behind your back. You will need to watch the players who do not have the ball as well as those who do. You may have to ignore the ball to watch elsewhere. There can be no getting a second wind, no coasting, but unremitting vigilance and intense concentration. You have got to be right or as near right as is humanly possible in your translation of the events that occur before you in terms of right and wrong, legal and illegal, acceptable and unacceptable. You will need a cool head, sound judgement, patience and firmness.

If you can do all this, you should finally command the players' confidence, from which will stem gradually their respect. Finally, if you are very lucky, and if you are very, very good, you will gain the admiration, perhaps even the affection, of the players.

41

Confidence will come from competence, just as respect will come from integrity. Once you achieve these, then violence will be well on the way to being absent from any game that you control. The boys will, of their own volition but with your help, have put away childish things and become men.

5

Developing Individual Skills

by C. M. ('NELIE') SMITH

> *Nelie Smith appeared nineteen times for South Africa, five times as captain. He became coach to the Orange Free State team in 1971 and coached the Springboks against the 1980 Lions. He has played and studied rugby in many parts of the world and in recent years has coached all races in the game in South Africa to help bring about multi-racial rugby.*

One of the main purposes of any coaching session is to put right the individual faults which the coach has observed. He must be able to read his players and rectify their mistakes. When he explains these faults to a player he must make it very, very simple, by explanation, by demonstration, imitation, direction and repetition.

However well a player may perform a particular skill, there is almost always room for improvement through this type of coaching, but never at the expense of individual flair. Only the truly natural players don't need to be coached – players like Mannetjies Roux. Mannetjies Roux was a centre who had a devastating break, change of pace and acceleration, but all the centres he played with said it was impossible to play with him because he was so unpredictable, although everyone agreed he was a genius. So Danie Craven got hold of a sprinter, made him a centre and told him, 'I don't want you just to play rugby, what I want you to do is to follow Mannetjies Roux.' So this sprinter followed Mannetjies Roux wherever he went on the field, and he too became a Junior Springbok because he was following a genius and he was not waiting for the genius to join up with him again. If you had changed Mannetjies Roux, obviously we would have lacked some rugby history in South Africa and we would never even have heard of a centre sprinter by the name of Danie Borrmann who was the player who actually followed Mannetjies Roux around the pitch.

Never forget the word 'individual' in the title of this chapter. It stimulates to praise where possible and if you are not too aggressive, the players will enjoy your coaching sessions more; this is of vital importance. A player is only too well aware if, through a misjudgement, he has cost you points on a Saturday, and he does not need you to be aggressive on the coaching field because of it. I have never sworn at a player. I have learned that, rather than being aggressive or insulting, you will get more out of your players if you insist that they work hard to rectify the fault. In other words I have demanded and got more through rectification and repetition than through insulting the player, because he is a human being, too.

In coaching the individual skills, be firm, be brief, demonstrate and ensure that everyone is active. Activity is vital – never let anyone stand along the touch line. The whole object of any session is to make it as enjoyable and as realistic as possible, even when you teach the skills, and ensure that it is game-related as well. It helps considerably to sub-divide the field into small areas, as the Welsh and the English do with their very good grid system. In South Africa, when we have our contact game we divide the forwards and backs separately and play in confined areas. The forwards play between the 22-metre line and the goal line and that teaches them to go forward all the time. The whole object is to keep the ball alive, using the technique and skill of each individual. The same applies to the backs. The execution of moves in a smaller area brings out their best skills because they simply must be able to do it. It is from these small beginnings that your sessions progress. Call it the progression pyramid. Always start with the simple things. Ensure that the players do the simple things well before moving on to the more complicated areas. That is where we as coaches sometimes fall down because we start with the complicated things first instead of the simple ones. It is our job to resolve the complexities into the simplicities.

You must always bear in mind the standard of the group which you are coaching. You will not work with beginners in the same way that you will work with International players and if you lose the interest of your players, then you will have failed as a coach.

You will find that aids used in the right manner will facilitate learning and help to maintain interest, but even more important is the use of rugby balls. I suggest one ball per four players because that means that four players are active; if there is only one ball for thirty players then the tallest chap gets all the coaching and all the enjoyment of that particular session. You will find that by using one ball between four players they not only enjoy themselves more but you get a higher work-rate from them.

Only certain muscles are used to perform any movement and that is why it is so important that we relate our coaching sessions to the game situation: because muscles need specific exercise and training to execute specific tasks. In a scrum a forward has to bind tightly, tightening and squeezing as hard as possible, so the muscles which are used to execute that specific task need to get that specific exercise. That is one reason why practice must be as realistic as possible, but another principle that governs the teaching of skills is that there must always be contact, pressure, opposition and competition. Repetition, too: ask a skilful player like Gerald Davies how he executed those devastating side-steps and he won't be able to answer because he is not used to having to think about performing that skill. It was an automatic action, an involuntary action, but polished through constant practice and repetition.

A few further points to remember. First, simplicity: as a coach you may want to make an impression on your players with some long talks on the field, but resist the temptation. You know where they went wrong and they will also know, especially at the higher levels, and you can discuss those points very firmly but briefly. Next, always teach skills when the players are mentally fresh. Don't start teaching skills when they are very tired. Variety in your programme during the season is also of vital importance. We had the experience recently of one of our provinces whose forwards formed basically the Test side for the Springboks that year. Their performance was suffering because they weren't mentally fit after a very heavy season. So when they came to play another province they decided not to have a heavy training session but just an hour's discussion on the Wednesday prior to the game, while the other side were still running up steep hills and doing press-ups. The side who were mentally prepared and mentally fit won 37-0. So mental preparation is of vital importance when you start teaching skills.

We in South Africa at school level, even at the beginning with boys aged eight in the scrum, do not play mini-rugby. We play fifteen-a-side rugby and we have those eight young forwards playing against opposition. We try to keep it very simple, and we find that even in the scrummage we can get an explosive shove forward by keeping it simple. Constant repetition is the essential thing, and it is surprising how much enjoyment these young boys get out of it, too.

The individual skills required of a forward are of course an integral part of his game, but in the forwards the tendency will be to concentrate more on unit skills which are dealt with elsewhere in this book. In the backs (while not neglecting their coaching as a unit), the emphasis may well be more on the skills of the individual. Backs *can* beat forwards, as has been proved in games where for eighty minutes a pack of forwards on one side were prepared to scrummage from one goal line to the other, while on the opposing sides the backs were always prepared to run the ball and keep possession and that managed to win the game.

Always remember that William Webb Ellis had a running and handling game in mind. He was frustrated by playing the ball with his feet so he picked that ball up and started to run with it, and that is the object of the game.

I will always accept the challenge to convert any kicking fly-half into a passing, running fly-half. By that I mean that any fly-half of International calibre should be able to distribute the ball well. There is no reason why he can't run the ball, and that is a bonus. If I have fifteen players in my side who can handle the ball then that is a bonus too, and I have got an advantage over any of my opponents. Why? Because another object of the game is to keep the ball alive: once the ball is in your possession there must be no stoppages until you have scored a try. This is called continuity, and you can't achieve it without skilled handling. Attacking rugby means good and scrupulous handling right along the back line and you must be able to teach your players to take any ball, no matter how difficult or unexpected it may be. Passing is a vital skill, and the difference in the Test matches between the two sides in New Zealand in 1971 was the passing ability of the British Lions. To see John Dawes pass, with an ability I have never seen on the rugby field before, was a revelation. His judgement, accuracy and swiftness of pass were supreme. Other skilful players on hand were Mike Gibson, Barry John, David Duckham and Gerald Davies, and it was in large measure due to their exceptional handling skills that the Lions beat the All Blacks in a Test series in New Zealand – always one of the great feats in rugby football.

Now one of the key factors when it comes to handling is to have

46

relaxed hands. If your fingers are stiff and you are tense, you are not able to handle the ball properly. Relax the fingers and your whole body will be relaxed, so you will be able to control any pass with all the ease in the world. When the players are achieving this relaxation, then you can say, 'Put that ball in front' and then 'Take it early'. In order to move the ball and take it into space we mustn't waste time. That means you put the ball in front, with finger-tip passing; it will move into the open spaces where you want it because the ball will beat the man. It is quicker than the man and that is also of vital importance. Continuing with the key factors, you swing the ball to your team-mate and you must watch where you are passing the ball; this is one of the simple things that we emphasise with the school-kids. Is there rhythm in the back line? Can the forwards handle like the backs – eight forwards who can handle like Frenchmen? You should always be trying to improve the skill of passing and receiving, the handling skill, because handling is the first pillar of rugby.

Rugby is also a running game and that's why we talk about the five 'S's' of the game: swing, straighten, slacken, sell and shoot, which sum up the skills of running, passing and handling followed by the dummy, the side-step, the swerve, the hand-off, change of pace and speed off the mark. One skill which has been neglected tremendously, and one which received priority in my day, was the dummy. I regard Hugo Porta of the Argentine as one of the best exponents of the dummy pass today and he is also a master in the art of passing. When it comes to the side-step, I think of Gerald Davies, David Duckham and Phil Bennett. This brings to mind the game between the Ba-Ba's and the All Blacks in 1973 when one of the most marvellous tries ever seen on the rugby field was scored. To me it was the combination of a team effort of individual skill, of sectional skill and of team skill, the like of which I have never seen in the game of rugby footbal before. There was Phil Bennett with those devastating side-steps; there was support from none other than the hooker, John Pullin, supporting back on his goal line, and then the supporting run of a player of the calibre of Gareth Edwards. Now if you watch that film closely, you will see that Gareth Edwards was almost in a static position on his own 22-metre line, but before the ball reached the halfway mark he was there to intercept the pass from Derek Quinnell to John Bevan and to score the best try ever scored in rugby as far as I am concerned. There was support through handling ability and the discipline of the side through its support work was there for all to see; not only was the side prepared to play going forward but also to play and to support when they were forced to go back.

The third individual skill is kicking. It is no use practising passing and running with the backs all the time because come Saturday afternoon, some of those backs are going to have to kick the ball and if they are going to do it well then they must practise the skills. They must master various types of kicking, which I call a foot-pass – the grubber kick, the chip kick, the up and under and also the cross kick in order to regain possession. It is also of vital importance for the players to communicate with each other on the field so that they will know exactly what is happening.

We also have to teach defence and the key factor for the tackled person: stay on your feet and make the ball available. The key factors for the tackler are: grip the opposition and turn him. Now when it comes to the tackle it is of great importance to know when to tackle and when not to tackle, and nowadays the law is very strict, especially when it comes to late tackles or early tackles. Rugby is a physically contested game which is why defence is of such importance, as is pressurising the opposition when they have the ball. Rugby is a 50% game – 50% attack, 50% defence – so you will have to defend for about forty minutes, pressurise the opposition, regain possession and capitalise on their mistakes.

Remember to use your wings, who are not necessarily supposed to be good handlers, to make the most of counterattack situations. About six years ago, when I was with the Free State, I coached a wing-threequarter who was so bad when it came to fielding the ball, especially a high kick, that in every match he was put under tremendous pressure because our opponents knew his weakness. However, we worked on his weakness and eventually he mastered the art of catching and fielding the high ball with the result that he still plays International rugby. The newspapers used to dwell on this weakness, and sometimes today we ask the newspapers to stress the point that he is still weak under the high ball because now he is the best counterattacker in South Africa. When he and a certain full-back play together, I would say that they are the best that I have seen in rugby football, and here is the opposition presenting the ball on a plate to this chap whose weakness is that he cannot catch the high ball!

Next there is the question of opposition. Your coaching must always progress through static, mild and active opposition. That means we have to apply pressure and then increase it, but sometimes we as coaches neglect the pressure aspect of the game, especially when we work with our backs. Backs like to call one move after another but there is no point in doing this if they cannot handle the ball properly, and to be able to handle the ball properly they must be able to do so under pressure. Technique must be put under severe pressure in order to make the player more skilful because he must make certain decisions on the field and, if he is not accustomed to making decisions, how can you say that he is one of your best players? If you have just an unopposed training session in the back line, passing the ball along the line, those players may all look like Internationals, but when they are put under pressure then they will start making mistakes because they must start making decisions. With pressure they will always make mistakes if they are not skilful players and, as Mike Gibson has so rightly stated, pressure produces skilful players.

When they give you a side to coach, don't say this is not my duty or that is not my duty. If you are set a task, then the end result is all that matters to those who appointed you as the coach. They are not going to tell you, 'You're a damned good coach, although we lost all our games. Your rucks were wonderful and your lineouts were wonderful and your threequarter play was a joy to see.' You have to look at all the facets of the game, including fitness, because you are the one who is going to be crucified at the end of the season, you are the one who is going to be fired upon if there is no end result. We in South Africa have some coaches who concentrate solely on the scrummage and although the score may be 50–0 against them, they are satisfied because they pushed the other side from one goal line to the other. That doesn't mean a thing. What really counts for the spectator is a winning side, make no mistake about it, and that is why we have to equip our players with the skills.

Let me end with a brief remark on the subject of violence. I can truthfully say that when it comes to violence in the game it is always the coaches that I will blame, and sometimes the referee. We should always coach both within the laws of the game and within the spirit of the game. If we select the players to play the game in the right spirit, then we will get an exhibition of rugby football, especially when executed by players of quality such as Gerald Davies, Phil Bennett, Mannetjies Roux, John Dawes, Barry John, Andy Irvine and Ollie Campbell. When I think of these and other world-class players, then I believe that rugby football has a long life ahead of it. Let's all be part of it.

6

Refereeing the Advantage Law and Positioning in Open Play

by ALAN HOSIE

Alan Hosie started refereeing at the age of 20. He was appointed to the Scottish International panel seven years later, but in 1971 had refereed Wales v. Canada at Cardiff. His first full International was in 1973 – Ireland v. England – and he has now had charge of numerous International matches and a considerable number of lesser representative games. He visited Canada in 1978 to have charge of the match against France at Calgary.

In the laws of rugby, Law 8, the advantage law, takes up only some seven lines in a book of seventy-eight pages. Even the notes take up only three paragraphs out of forty-five pages of notes. Yet no other law attracts so much discussion about its interpretation.

Despite this, I don't believe that anyone can teach a referee how to play the advantage law on the field of play. It is a feeling towards the game and a sympathetic approach towards the players who are participating on the park which are the essential factors. There can't be anything better from a refereeing point of view than to see an advantage played to the full with a try resulting at the end of it. Nothing would give me more pleasure, after having played the advantage and seen it work out well that way, than to go back to the point of the original infringement, give two fingers to the spectators who had been shouting for a scrum or penalty at the time of the infringement and say, 'There you are – you can have your scrum instead of the score!'

The history of the advantage law is very interesting, in that originally it was the non-offending captain who used to decide whether he wanted the game to go on because his team had gained an advantage after an infringement by the opposing team. So one way of applying the law might be to put yourself in the non-offending captain's position and ask yourself the question on the field of play: would I want play to continue, or would I say, 'No thanks, referee – please blow for the infringement'? There are only three occasions where the law is not applicable, and these are very minor ones: the ball or the ball-carrier touching the referee; the ball coming out of the tunnel in a scrummage situation; and the accidental off-side. At all other times the application of the advantage law is at the sole discretion of the referee, and it doesn't matter if this referee and that referee disagree; whatever the match referee decides in a particular situation is by definition the correct application of the law for that situation in that game. The important point is apply the advantage law consistently throughout the eighty minutes.

You can't put a defining time limit on how long you wait in your advantage interpretation. You, as the man with the whistle, are the sole judge of that during the game. There are those who blow up the instant an infringement occurs which affects adversely the play of the other side. For myself, I try to play advantage as long as possible without losing what was the thread of the original infringement, to see if the non-offending side do capitalise on the errors of their opponent. Only if they do not, then and only then would I blow for the infringement. If you think about it, if a referee blows immediately after the infringement occurs, he prevents further play, destroys any form of continuity and obviously on many occasions prevents the non-offending team from gaining an advantage. So it is important to assess situations quickly in the context of the game and make every endeavour to keep play moving at all times. Similarly, it is dangerous to talk in distances and the law tends never to be dogmatic in these respects, but I will stick my neck out and say this: if as a player I didn't gain twenty metres as an absolute minimum, then I would sooner that you as referee went back and gave me the advantage of a scrum or penalty kick. Just to dribble the ball five metres and to be told, 'All right, you've gone a little nearer the opponents' goal line', as opposed to getting a penalty kick, is a pretty skinny reward.

However, the law quite clearly says that there must be either a territorial advantage *or a tactical advantage*, and the tactical possession might be defined as something that would give more than the average possibility of a try being scored. But through how many pairs of hands will you allow the ball to travel before you deem the advantage to have been taken? Just what exactly constitutes a tactical advantage? Is it that our interpretation of the words, 'a fair opportunity to gain advantage', is not adequate? Is it that our interpretation of that is in fact out of step with the original intention of the law?

Think of some of these situations. A player comes off-side and is noticed by the referee. The referee plays advantage and a non-offending player attempts to kick to touch but does not find touch. What would you do? Would I bring back the play for a penalty? Yes, I would. Or take another situation of a player being off-side, and the ball goes through three or four players in a handling movement all along the line, but it only goes forward a distance of five or ten metres before the movement breaks down or there is a tackle. Would I say there has been no advantage there at all and bring play back for the penalty? Yes, I would. It would have been great if the attacking side could have scored six points, but the fact that their winger was brought down a yard from the line is not my fault; I have played my part in helping play to continue. Or take yet another example of a player being off-side near the goal line, and an attacking player takes a quick snap drop at goal and misses. Would I bring back play for the penalty award? Yes, I would.

The question is, in those situations am I giving a double advantage? There are those who would say that I am, and that it is a sign of weakness in a referee to say, 'Well, I'll leave it to see how far it will go, and if it doesn't come off then I'll pull it back and give a penalty.' If it comes off, the referee gets applause from the crowd for his playing of advantage. If it doesn't come off, he can always come back and give the penalty and be doubly safe, and the crowd will still say, 'Yes, he was right, he spotted that.'

There is also the school of thought which says that if the non-offending side loses the advantage through their own actions (for example, a missed touch-kick or drop-goal, or a kick ahead), then they should not be given a second bite of the cherry. But in the three examples I quoted above, I do not believe I am giving a double advantage. Surely the emphasis, within the framework of the law, is on scoring points, and this to me means tries as well as penalty kicks (our future interpretation of advantage might be helped by the further reduction of the value of the penalty goal and the increase in the value of the try). I would give the non-offending side the maximum opportunity; if we don't give them the opportunity to take the advantage, then how will the advantage arise in the first place? I would extend this even to acts of foul play or misconduct as long as the advantage is very obvious. While aware that it can upset players, I would still try to play the advantage law in these circumstances and at the next stoppage have words with the offending party. It could mean the difference between three and six points.

What about the situation where the referee is encouraging a player to play advantage even when he doesn't want to? Take the two-handed catch in the lineout, when the side catching the ball snap down and hold it. The whole reason that they hold it is to catch someone off-side. They are not interested in the advantage there, they want a penalty. Why is the ball held in the back of the scrum? Why does a scrum-half dummy the ball away or run away from the scrum? He doesn't want the advantage, he wants the penalty kick, and many referees feel obliged to give the penalty kick straightaway rather than waiting to see if an advantage develops, as I would do. Unless we give Law 8 a chance in such a situation, we might just as well delete it from the book entirely, and that would be the worst thing that we could ever do.

Your interpretation of the advantage law should not be governed in any way whatsoever by where the infringement happened. It is possible for a side to score from their own goal line, so even in defence situations I like to play the advantage if at all possible in order to achieve consistency. Similarly, the individual talent on display should not affect your decision. Mr X might be a wonderful kicker but that shouldn't really sway you in trying to interpret the advantage law uniformly during the entire eighty minutes.

I am a great believer in saying to the players aloud, as I keep going with play, that I am playing advantage. Where the indication of advantage is concerned, though, the golden rule in a game of rugby football is that at all times the players are expected to play the whistle. In the case of knock-ons etc, there is no need to indicate any form of advantage whatsoever. If, however, it is an offence which would warrant a penalty kick, then I have no objection whatsoever to the quick pointing action, which helps me and tells the players who are looking at me, the spectators and perhaps the media, who are part and parcel of the game now, that I have in fact seen an infringement and am playing advantage. I don't go along with the guy with his hand up in the air, running around as if saying, 'May I leave the room, please?' but I have no objection to the quick pointing action.

The one thing that horrifies me from time to time is referees going to the point of infringement, remaining there and waiting to see if any advantage occurs. If it does and play continues, they have already been isolated by some considerable distance and it takes them quite a time to get back up with the play again. So take a quick note of where the infringement took place on the field, but don't remain there, follow play. If in fact play breaks down and there is no advantage, you have a mental note of where the infringement took place and you can go back to the spot.

So there is the advantage law, a great law, the best in the book with the fewest words. It is there to assist the game and those who play the game, and if we can get some degree of continuity then the players must be happy. Use the advantage law as liberally as possible in a sympathetic and understanding way, with a feeling for the players, and you will have succeeded tremendously in benefiting the game while remaining the thirty-first player on the park.

Moving on to the second topic of this chapter, positioning in general play, the individuality of the man with the whistle is very, very important. No two of us are alike, each with his own thoughts, his own attitudes. The basic essential is to get to the breakdown of play quickly and, once there, to ensure that the ball is next played within the framework of the laws. One only has to look at Laws 18 and 19 to realise how important it is to be on the scene, and quickly. Is it a tackle or is it not? If not, how may the ball next be played within the framework of the laws? That is why it is so important to have the player carrying the ball in sight at all possible times, as well as those players in his immediate vicinity.

Positioning at the lineout, scrummage, ruck and maul will be dealt with in later chapters, but in general play, you want to be on a line parallel with the ball or the ball-carrier. In my opinion it is better to be ten or fifteen metres away but in line, rather than five metres away but behind; in fact, it can even be beneficial to be very slightly in front of the ball. Rugby is not a static game, so you cannot really afford to remain still at any time during the eighty minutes. Whatever general position you adopt, it is important to feel comfortable and confident that you personally can from that position best judge the game by getting a clear view of it in all places. It is in general play more than any other time during the game where your own speed, your own height and your own agility will have an important bearing on exactly where you run.

To look at a few specific points, at the kick-off one often sees a referee take up his position in the middle, but before the ball has been kicked off he has run over the halfway line and is maybe two or three yards in front of the kicker before the kick has been taken. It only needs a reverse kick and within seconds of play beginning we have the embarrassing situation of the ball having hit the referee. So if you stand in the middle of the park beside the kicker, then by all means stay beside him, but don't interfere with him, which means remaining behind him. Conversely, I don't like the referee standing between the forwards and the kicker, because he has got to look one way to see the ball being kicked and the other to make sure the players are behind the kicker when the kick is taken, and that really is not very easy. The third position that I do from time to time use, but only from time to time, is on the touch line when a kick-off is being taken. The only problem is that you have got to be very alert to the guy taking the kick the wrong way, because you can become isolated.

One of the things that I like to do before a match is to tell my touch judges that if a penalty kick at goal misses, doesn't go over the dead-ball line and is caught in-goal, then play is still in progress, and in these situations I like my touch judges to remain at the posts, thereby becoming part of the posts as far as the laws of the game are concerned. They will not interfere, and I will cover the touch lines. The other thing is, when a penalty kick is being taken, I try to stand as near as I can to the kicker so that I have a line on the ball through the posts and it will be my decision, not the touch judges', whether the ball is in or out. Where short penalty kicks are concerned, there are so many moves now that one wonders frankly what is coming next, and you never know really where the kick is going to be taken or what ploy is going to happen. A couple of seasons ago, I started to adopt a position ten metres in front of the place where the kick has been awarded; there, I am not interfering in any way with the kicker or his ploys. The only thing that you can miss there would be a forward pass which of course could be important – forward passes are always important – but you are eliminating the problem of getting in the way. If you prefer to remain where the penalty kick is being taken, then stay close to the guy who takes the kick, because that way you are unlikely to interfere very much.

One last aspect of positioning is that magic area very near to the goal line or in fact in-goal. This is the area where so much can happen and it will always happen so quickly. The position you must adopt at all times near the goal line is on the in-goal side of play.

7

Coaching the Scrum

by CARLOS VILLEGAS

> *Carlos Villegas is the outstanding coach in Argentinian rugby and for many years has been coach to the Argentine national team. He is also coach to the San Isidro Club. During his playing career he was an outstanding forward and leader.*

I have divided this chapter into three sections, beginning with the one which is the most important because with full comprehension of it the rest becomes almost unnecessary. That first part is the philosophy of the scrum. The second part will deal with the main scrum formations in the different stages of development in our game. The third part will deal with the techniques that can be applied in the scrum.

PHILOSOPHY OF THE SCRUM

The scrum is not just one more thing in our game. Together with the tackle, it is one of the two distinctive features of rugby. We know of other games in which the ball is either passed or kicked and players jump for it, run with it and struggle for it more or less roughly. There are other aspects of rugby which may have some similarities with other sports, but the scrum is the one formation in our game which is peculiar to rugby. Nor is it just a technical aspect of the game: it is mainly a means of disciplining the group of players that form the pack of forwards. The scrum should therefore be considered by coaches as a means and not as an end, because a forward's value to the team depends on his ability to add his strength to that of his pack and there is nowhere better than the scrum to learn to put this idea into practice. This discipline is absolutely basic in rugby, not only in the scrum itself but also in other parts of the game such as mauls, rucks, lineouts, drop-outs, kick-offs. Not only is such discipline necessary for forwards, but the backs should be well aware of it and of the great effort that the forwards put into getting the ball with the obvious benefit that this means for the whole team.

The set scrum has certain pecularities which make it quite different from other parts of the game. For instance, it is the only part of the game in which players are in physical contact before the ball is in play. This gives the scrum a very special flavour and is very important because of its psychological effect on the rest of the game. Its importance is reflected in the common saying that front-row forwards form a sort of family or clan. One of the reasons may very well be that these six players from both front rows play the game a few seconds more than the rest of the players because they are in contact, physical contact, before the ball is put in. Every rugby coach should have this thought in mind before starting any tactical or technical teaching of the scrum.

The true spirit of rugby football, in relation to the scrum, means a lot more than just getting possession of the ball. In other words, the scrum is not formed just to get the ball into play after a minor infringement; that could be done more easily by a formation of three men from each side in front of each other, or simply by giving the ball to the side not responsible for the stoppage of play and thus avoiding the tremendous struggle and pressure by the eight forwards of each side. Nor is it true, although it is very commonly and wrongly believed in the rugby world, that the team putting the ball into the scrum is the one that should finally get it. If that were so, it would be a lot easier to give the ball to the team not responsible for the stoppage of play and make the opposite team fall back to an agreed distance, and then by just touching the ball with the foot it would be in play once again. As it is, the only advantage given to the team not responsible for the stoppage is the slight one of putting the ball into the scrum from that side where the hooker is closer to the scrum-half, but by no means does the spirit of the game demand that the other team has to give up any hope of getting the ball from that particular scrum. The scrum, then, is the very beginning of the battle between the forwards to get the ball, a battle which later continues with lineouts, mauls, rucks and in the loose.

What all this means is that the scrum is not just a fight for the ball; it is the winning of the scrum itself that is of great importance, and the winning of the ball is only part of this battle. So what is the real meaning of winning the scrum? The real meaning of winning the scrum is not only getting the ball but pushing back the gain line and the off-side line and defeating the opposite side physically and psychologically. Then when we win the ball it is a good ball, and if we lose the ball we have still won the scrum because what the opposition will have is bad ball that is unlikely to produce any benefit for them.

Once you understand that it is possible to win a scrum without gaining possession of the ball, the significance of the scrum as a symbol of team-work becomes clearer: it is a concentration of effort by a group of players and not the action of just one player, the hooker, no matter how great his ability may be. That group of players includes the scrum-half, who should be considered as the ninth member of the pack. He should live and understand the philosophy of the scrum, and the act of putting in the ball must be part of the effort that eight players, and with him nine, are making together. All the same, to quote the RFU book, *Why the Whistle Went*, 'obtaining the ball from a scrum should be a consequence of the honest pushing of a pack of forwards rather than the consequence of a trick between the hooker and the scrum-half.'

All great thinkers about rugby acknowledge the pre-eminence of the scrum. Dr Danie Craven of South Africa has said, 'Everything starts in the set scrum' and Mr Francisco Cambo, a well-known coach in my country, wrote, 'The scrum is the foundation of forward play', which is equivalent to saying that the scrum is the foundation of the rugby game. We all remember the successful tours of the Lions to New Zealand in 1971, coached by Carwyn James, and to South Africa in 1974, coached by Syd Millar: in both cases their good scrummaging was a basic factor in their success. I remember a tour I made to Wales in 1972 with the San Isidro Club. Ray Williams paid us a visit at the Afan Lido and was asked which was the more important ball to get in a match, whether it was from the lineout because the backs were twenty yards apart, or from the rucks and mauls because of the variety of attacking moves that could be started from those situations. Ray answered, 'None of those. The most important ball to get is from the set scrum,' and went on to say, 'The scrum exerts an influence on the lineout and also the mauls and rucks, whereas these situations have no influence on the scrum.' After the French tour to Argentina in 1974, when they won all their seven matches brilliantly, their coach and my good friend, Jean Descleau, said, 'On this tour we have learned that the most brilliant attack can be countered by great scrummaging.' He was referring to the great difficulty that his team had in beating the Pumas in the second Test, which they won by 31 points to 27. Remember, too, the tremendous effectiveness of the scrummaging power of the French team that won the Five Nations Championship in 1977 without having a try scored against them. They say that New Zealand pay no proper attention to the set scrums, but just read the chapters on scrummaging in *Fred Allen on Rugby* and in *Team Rugby* by J. J. Stewart.

Techniques and tactics are of course necessary, but the results will be a lot better if we apply them within the philosophy of the scrum which can be summarised thus:

1   Use the scrum as a means and not as an end.
2   Use the scrum to discipline the players, forwards and backs.
3   Use the scrum to educate the players in team-work, forwards and backs.

SCRUM FORMATIONS

We must start by analysing a formation which is no longer used, not because of its inefficiency but because of changes in the laws of rugby. The understanding of this formation will help us to underline concepts which are still valid and which will be valid as long as this game is played. I refer to the famous 2-3-2 formation of the All Blacks in 1905, which was very successful during a tour of Great Britain. This formation (Fig. 1) consisted of two players in the front row, three players in the second row and two players in the third row: total seven players. They used one man to put in the ball and a different man to collect the ball from the scrum and pass it to the backs. This formation produced excellent team-work and a better concentration of strength than the 3-2-3 formation that was used at the time and for many years after in British rugby and in the rest of the world. This concentration of strength was possible because of a better distribution of the forwards in the scrum and stronger support to the front row. Since according to the laws at that time the front-row players were absolutely free to place their heads as they pleased, by adopting the formation in Fig. 2 the All Blacks were able to leave more than half of the British pack out of the game. They bound on the opposing props, putting up to five opposing forwards out of the game.

60

Fig. 1

This method of forming a scrum showed an intelligent approach to the game and has left us a lot of experience which can still be applied. Although a 2-3-2 formation could no longer be used when the laws established that the front row had to be formed by three men placing their heads alternately with those of their opposite numbers, there are various formations in use today, and further possible variants exist to make this game more interesting than it already is. The 3-2-3 formation (Figs. 3 and 3a) was used for many years throughout the world, and permitted easy hooking of the ball between the prop and the lock without the interference of the flanker. However, the biggest advantage of this formation was the use of the wheel in attack. This is one aspect of the game which has been neglected and is no longer much used because coaches consider it an old system. But it can

Fig. 2

still be a very efficient attacking way to reach the gain line, even if it is very difficult to carry out properly – difficult, but not impossible.

The 3-2-3 formation lacks support for the front row compared with the more recent 3-4-1 formation (Fig. 4), which gives a wonderful opportunity for concentration of strength on the hooker. In this it is very like the All Blacks' 2-3-2, but they obtained the same, or maybe better, results using seven forwards, whereas we have to use eight.

The other formation which is also used nowadays is a 3-3-2 formation, with the right flanker no. 7 packing between left flanker no. 6 and left lock no. 4, or the left flanker no. 6 packing between right flanker no. 7 and right lock no. 5. This alternative is very useful, particularly when the scrum is taking place near to the touch line: by switching your blind-side flanker to the third row and bringing him over to the open side, you are helping to turn the scrum, thus bringing your back row towards the gain line and setting up a platform for a move close to the scrum. This 3-3-2 formation is a tactical formation and should be used during the game only on certain occasions and not throughout.

Fig. 3

Fig. 3a

Fig. 4

Remember always to use your imagination to produce different formations within the law according to your needs and the different situations in the game.

SCRUMMAGING TECHNIQUES

Here we are dealing with a tremendously broad subject, full of details, but there are priorities which we have to remember whilst training a scrum. A friend of mine in Argentina used to say when talking about rugby and in particular the scrum, 'We must never, in teaching this game or during a rugby talk, allow a single tree to obscure the view of the whole forest.' In other words, a minor detail should not stop us from advancing in the analysis of this part of the game.

Let us now further divide the technical teaching of the scrum into two sub-sections: the scrum as a static formation (the actual forming of the scrum before the putting in of the ball) and a dynamic formation (the general attitude of the whole pack at the moment when the ball is put into the scrum). In the first part we have to consider four major points: perfect binding between the forwards; backs in a straight position and parallel to the ground; flexion of the legs in the correct way; and positioning of the feet.

Perfect binding between the forwards. This skill has to be acquired by practical and detailed teaching, seeking as a final objective the greatest co-ordination between all the forwards and the maximum concentration of strength on the hooker. Here we

Fig. 5

have one basic principle of the scrum, which is that before pushing forwards the pack must press inwards towards the centre of the scrum, or in other words, compress the scrum so as to obtain as complete a unit as possible. Fig. 5 shows the front row as a unit in itself. The shoulders of the props must be completely inserted below the armpits of the hooker and at the same time the hooker must bind under the armpits of his props, if possible not just grabbing their shirts but also with the tips of his fingers pressing inwards on the armpits of his props. The front row *must* form a closely-knit unit to provide the necessary foundation for a first-class scrum.

The same principle of unity applies, of course, to the locks, as shown in Fig. 6. These locks must also have a perfect interlacing with the front row because they are mainly responsible for the hips of the front-row players remaining as close together as possible. There are two different opinions on this. One maintains that the locks should bind on the front row with their hands

Fig. 6

between the legs of the props and grabbing their shorts as shown in Fig. 7. This system ensures that the lock will never slip over the hips or back of the prop. The second opinion maintains that the locks should bind around the hips of the props with their arms (Fig. 8). In this case the lock contributes much more to the consolidation of the front row, and although both systems have advantages and disadvantages, I prefer the second alternative: the close unity of the front row is of paramount importance and with adequate practice of this binding, the lock does not necessarily have to slip over the hips or back of his prop.

Flankers have to remember above all else that they form part of the second row of the scrum and that while the scrum is taking place their job is exactly the same as that of the locks – to support their front row hard and continually. A flanker should also pack as parallel as possible to his lock to transmit the greatest strength to the front row. This is opposed to the traditional concept of the open flanker trying to give more protection to his scrum-half, but

Fig. 7

it increases the power that the eight forwards can apply to the scrum to provide the best possible quality of ball. In other words, I strongly believe that the best protection that can be given to a scrum-half is the quality of the possession that he receives. The flanker should place his outside hand on the ground to provide additional balance which in turn will produce more strength when pushing. It also stops him gripping his prop, which is uncomfortable for that player.

The no. 8 is the real helmsman of the scrum and his responsibility is to consolidate and bind his locks, while supporting the rest of his fellows from behind.

Straight backs.   It must be clearly understood that the only way of transmitting power in the scrum is with a straight back and with the head up, well up (Fig. 9). The scrum as a system of transmission of force is more efficient when the backs are kept straight:

Fig. 8

Fig. 9

Fig. 10

the front row must transmit the strength coming from the players pushing from behind, as the locks must do with the no. 8's strength. In Fig. 10 you can see all the strength being transmitted by one forward's back to his opponent, who, with his back bent and his head down, is not only receiving all the strength from the opposite forward but has also lost his arm strength. This makes the player feel tired both physically and mentally and this pressure increases throughout the match. He's not unfit: he lacks technical support, not physical training.

Leg flexion.   This is a basic element in generating power. The most powerful parts of the human body are the thighs and the legs, so if we can make good use of them during the scrum the results are going to be better. The knees have to be flexed so that they can straighten when the ball is put into the scrum; this is the dynamic moment of the scrum. Straight legs in the scrum are useful to avoid going backwards, but they are useless to produce additional strength, as normally should happen once the ball is put in. On the other hand, excessively bent knees make it difficult to move the body forwards. Fig. 11 shows the ideal position of the legs: the thigh remains perpendicular to the ground while head and hips are more or less at the same level. This would be the ideal position for the pack before the ball is put in. Adequate

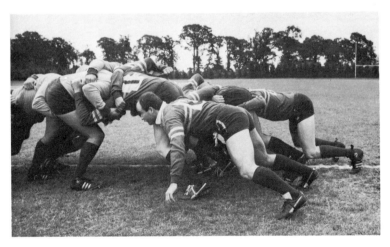

Fig. 11

studs are needed to obtain the correct grip of the ground and the proper position of the feet.

Foot positions. There is an enormous variety of positions, depending on which type of scrummaging you are using. Fig. 12 shows the conventional system.

Now look at Fig. 13, which shows the positioning by Francisco Cambo and called in Argentina the Cambo system. It is fundamental that each forward places each foot in a position that allows the forward behind him to be comfortable so that he can produce his strength in the most positive way to achieve a maximum concentration of strength on the hooker. In the Cambo system, therefore, both feet of the hooker are almost in the same line, as are the two inside feet of the props; this way the

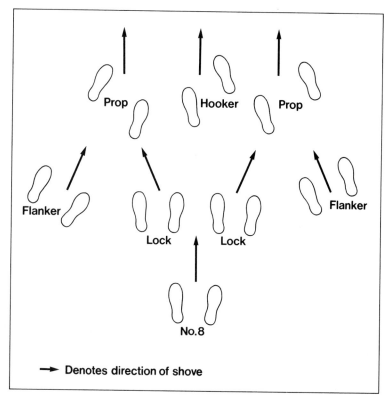

Fig. 12

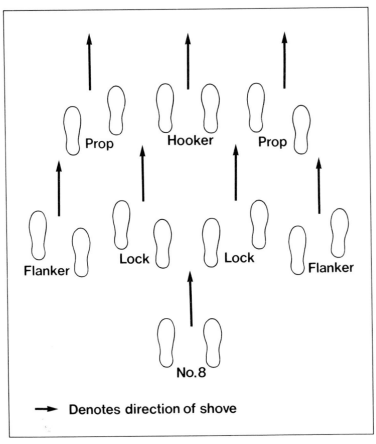

Fig. 13

buttocks of the props and hooker are offered to the locks in a way that enables them to push harder. In the same way the outside foot of the prop is behind, in order to offer his buttocks to the flanker. The locks place their inside feet slightly behind the outside ones, so the no. 8 can push on their inside buttocks. We could obtain greater power from the locks if they placed their feet at the same level more or less, or if they placed their outside feet behind the inside feet, but this system does use the complete and correct power coming from the no. 8. The position of the lock with his inside feet back also allows free space which can be used for keeping the ball in case of a push-over try.

All the different ways of positioning the feet look for channels which allow better heeling of the ball (see Fig. 14). Channel 1 is for the very quick heel, which counters the push from the opposing pack. It will not be good ball if it touches the feet of the prop or flanker because of the push of the opposing forwards, and the scrum-half lacks protection, but channel 1 will always be useful providing the push from the pack is sufficient to hold the opposition.

Channel 2, through the legs of the no. 8, gives rather slower possession of the ball but better protection of the scrum-half. Remember that quick ball is not everything: we must aim for good ball and good ball means that our scrum-half has room to play the ball without pressure.

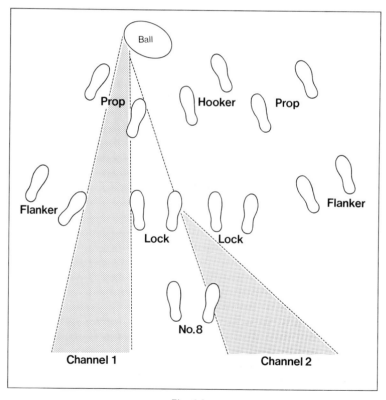

Fig. 14

But more important than the use of either of these channels is the positioning of your forwards' feet to maximise the power that they can produce when packing properly. For example, I want the flankers as close as possible to the locks' hips, pushing parallel with them in order not to lose strength, even though this restricts the use of channel 1 unless my pack is moving forward. Similarly, the loose-head prop using the Cambo system of foot positioning has to use his head and body to protect his hooker from the opposing tight-head's pressure, but you can be sure that he is in exactly the right position to exert maximum force.

Let us imagine now that the ball is in the scrum, the forwards have flexed their legs and thrown their bodies forward. There are now two possibilities: either for the hooker to advance his right foot and hook the ball, or a continuous eight-man shove and then the right foot of the tight-head prop hooks the ball. In the latter case channel 1 and channel 2 only are used, always with the pack going forward. It provides slower possession but good protection for the scrum-half, and pushes back the gain line and off-side line.

To achieve the eight-man shove, after flexing the legs and throwing the body forward, a sharp extension of the sixteen legs must follow as the ball is put in, without any foot moving from its original position and without the scrum advancing before the ball touches the ground. This is very difficult to do but the nearer you get to it, the nearer you will be to better and more effective scrummaging. You will get good ball – not quick ball, good ball – and at the same time will have a destructive effect on the opposite pack. The eight-man shove is particularly recommended when the ball is put in by the opposition – you *can* win the ball without hooking.

Last, but very important for the dynamic part of the scrum, there is the putting of the ball into the scrum by the ninth member of the pack, the scrum-half. According to the laws, the ball must be seen previous to the put-in by both packs, more or less midway between the scrum-half's ankles and knees. Even well-known scrum-halves at International level do not give enough importance to this skill of the put-in, and do not feel themselves to be the ninth forward.

The team putting in the ball has only two advantages under the law: its hooker is closer to the ball than the opposite side's, and it has the choice of the moment to put the ball in. Talking about that moment, either the scrum-half tells the pack when the ball is coming in, which is effective providing the pack is ready and prepared to receive this ball, or the hooker or scrum-leader gives the order for the put-in and this is also very efficient. But the order can be given by the ball itself. In other words, when the scrum-half holds the ball midway between the knee and the ankle, showing it to the forwards, the forwards must look at the ball and follow its movement. This is very difficult to do but it has the big advantage that you are not giving an order to your own pack which is thus communicated to the opposite forwards as well.

My final word is a reminder that in scrummaging you have a lot of possibilities. You must use your imagination and use different types of scrummaging. Don't spend your time watching and criticising the system of other clubs: use your own system. If you do not, you are not progressing, especially in a part of the game which gives so much freedom for the different use of the forwards' feet, arms and shoulders.

8

Refereeing the Scrum

by ALAN WELSBY

Alan Welsby teaches at Manchester GS, where he is the Director of PE, and has been there for nineteen years. After enforced retirement as a player due to a rib injury, he joined the Manchester Referees' Society and after nine years was elected onto the RFU list. Two years later he was placed on the RFU A1 list. He has refereed every major touring side to visit the UK and regards his most important match as the Grand Slam game, Wales v. France at Cardiff in 1978.

What is the scrummage? There is the story that is told of a PE master who at the last minute had to go in and take an English class. He finished up talking about definitions, rugby definitions. One of the questions that he asked the class of 11-year-olds was: what is a rugby scrum? One rather weedy, bespectacled little boy was obviously not going to become involved in physical contact sports, but he desperately wanted to take part and not to be outdone, he quietly got hold of a dictionary, looked in it, and then stretched his arm and said, 'Sir, Sir!' His time came and quite unashamedly he stood up, produced his dictionary, opened it up and read: 'Impurities which rise to the top of a liquid when it is boiled or fermented; persons of dirty, vicious or criminal habits.'

Unfortunately, this young lad had not realised that the words 'scrum' and 'scum' were on the same page, and of course he had just focused his eyes on 'scum' by mistake. What he should have said was: 'A struggle between forwards of both teams who contest the ball on the ground which is between them.'

Now I must say that I like the best of both worlds, and with a little journalistic licence came up with a combination of the two definitions: 'A struggle between forwards of both teams for a ball which is on the ground, and which if not adequately controlled by the referee will ferment and will almost certainly cause the persons involved to resort to dirty, vicious or criminal habits.'

Of course there are other definitions, and you might prefer the International Board's version of Law 20 or even the more technical version accredited to a coach – 'where one is made aware of the unit skill, made up of individual skills which are each linked and interlocked into one efficient force, as the players attempt to win the ball which is put into the scrummage between them' – but whatever your preference, there is no mistaking the fact that this is an important phase of play, because of the frequency with which it occurs in the game; because it is a bruising, bodily contact situation; because it is a unit made up of different individuals all of whom have different characters and temperaments; and because it is formed and contested in a closely bound, rather undignified position near the ground. It does need to be controlled with firmness from the beginning. Firmness and fairness. Otherwise those impurities will spread to the other phases of our game where the shape of play is similar to that of the scrum and where vengeance can perhaps more easily be extracted by the aggrieved player – the ruck and the maul.

There are those who say that the game is won or lost in the front row of the scrummage. The referee's game is won or lost in the front row, too, and if he is not able to control it in a way that is not only fair but also acceptable to the players, then he is in trouble and the rucks and the mauls will be that much more difficult to handle. You do yourself a favour and everyone in the game a favour if you control the front row right from the start.

Now the laws governing the scrummage are fairly straightforward: it is a means of bringing the ball back into play in the field of play, it must be contested by at least five players of each team at the place of infringement, stationary prior to the put-in, and all these players must be correctly bound up. Players will expect you to make sure that there is a tunnel, that feet are not illegally crossed, and that any unbinding player does so within the law. They will also expect the scrummage to be square so that they can make an effective forward push. Now surely that is not too difficult!

It often happens that quite early on in the game a referee is persuaded to bend a little in the interest of flow rather than fairness, or to put it another way, he doesn't particularly like to be seen blowing the whistle yet again so early on in the match. So he ignores the off-square scrummage which is being marginally turned in favour of the non-putting-in team, the manicuring flanker as he tries to disrupt the signals that the hooker has a perfect right to make with his hand, the off-straight put-in, the break backwards by the flanker from a position in front of the ball, the crab, the wheel, the untimely shove. That referee is thinking about the wrong image: not that of the scrum but rather that of himself. Or he sincerely believes that he is doing the game a service by allowing the play to continue, and because he appears to have got away with it and flowing play seems to continue without the slightest form of mayhem or aggravation, he wrongly concludes that he has made the right decision. Of course no referee wants to appear whistle-happy at the start of a big occasion, and every referee prays for a quiet start, but if the referee doesn't sort things out fairly, then the players will do so unfairly. Even if he gets away with it at the first scrum, or even the second or third, his card will have been marked by the players and he will have it all to answer for later on in the game.

In the 1978/79 season I was given the All Blacks' third game, the one they called the fifth Test, at Swansea against West Wales. They hit each other so hard when they went down for the first scrummage that you could hear the crack way outside the ground. They didn't flinch as they went down or as they waited for the ball to be put in, and the spectators high up on the terrace could have been forgiven for wondering why the whistle went, but if I'd let that go on – head against head, arching upwards as they collided and meshed – I would have had mayhem long before the first lineout took place. In fact I penalised West Wales because, having come to the mark, they then retreated a little in order to gain that dangerously unfair advantage and momentum before charging into the scrum. To have just left it at that would have been far too risky, even if I hadn't heard the mutterings of what was going to happen next time they came together, so the next time the whistle went for a scrummage I was there before they got down and in a position to give them a little piece of advice. I think it is called preventive refereeing, and it has a very important role to play. Quite often the players will appreciate and accept a word rather than the whistle, and anything you can do to foster that kind of attitude can only be to your eventual advantage, but when this considerate approach is not heeded, then you really must be firm, even if it does mean blowing the whistle yet again and possibly upsetting those sporting graduates who sit warmly wrapped in the shelter of the Press box.

Collapsing is not only irritating, it is dangerous to life and limb; to collapse the scrum deliberately is against the law, but a penalty kick is a futile gesture against the possibility of a broken neck. It is a fact that a collapsed scrummage can cause irreparable damage, and there are players lying in hospital who are ample testimony. That a player can be so injured in an accident is most unfortunate; that it should be the result of a deliberate act is unforgivable. We must all act to eliminate this kind of behaviour within the game.

John Silvers, a consultant surgeon at Stoke Mandeville paraplegic centre, has this to say about scrummaging and forward behaviour, when describing the injuries of some of his patients who happen to be rugby players: 'Seven of my patients broke their necks in the front row of the scrummage. Two were hookers whose heads were locked tight when the scrum collapsed, and five were props. It must be appreciated that great shearing strains and forces are exerted on the neck in a collapsed scrum. There is very great danger to those involved. One player said that the scrums were coming together far too quickly, and that they did not mesh properly so that his head was forced outwards and downwards. Another said that he was propping against a much shorter fellow, who was far less experienced than himself. Consequently, although he was more experienced, or rather because he was more experienced, the scrum opposite him collapsed.' So experience is important, and sheer physical size, or lack of it, must be taken into consideration when trying to apportion the blame.

At the highest level in the game, any such weaknesses can no doubt be neutralised by the action of the other members of the unit, but at a slightly lower level this kind of compensation may be missing, and that is when the collapsing scrum is at its most dangerous, particularly when the engine room, the second row, keep up their shove and quite deliberately bury all beneath them. In such a case, don't allow players to unfold without so much as a word to them, in the mistaken belief that having experienced the bruising pressure of the screw and the collapse the players will be less likely to do it again. A top-class referee who fails in this respect is helping to determine a pattern of rugby scrummaging that will spread to every quarter of the land, and unfortunately, many of the players and referees involved at the lower levels will not have the experience to deal with the situation as the law demands.

In Dr Silvers' opinion there are two recognised manoeuvres in rugby scrummaging these days:

1 The charging in of packs in an effort to intimidate the opposition
2 The collapsing of the scrum when possession is vital.

Both, he says, are preventable and if so, why do they still go on? Regular and consistent enforcement of the existing law, plus a fuller understanding by the players and referees of the consequences of this kind of dangerous play, will give considerable protection. There is nothing wrong with existing law, so enforce it. If you bend when you see this kind of thing going on in front of you, you are just as responsible for any subsequent injury as the players themselves. There is nothing wrong with scrummaging law, nor has there been; it has always been a case of permissive refereeing. It is that as much as the change in playing attitudes that has caused many of the unwelcome and dangerous aspects of scrummaging to materialise.

Knowing and understanding the players' role is vital for those who wish to referee at the highest level, and if you can get this message across to the players it is bound to have a psychological impact and work favourably for you on the field. Take for example this question of collapsing the scrummage, or of crabbing before the put-in: two manoeuvres deliberately engineered either to deprive the opposition of a score or to secure possession against the stronger push, or simply to disrupt or unsettle opponents at any stage of the scrummage. How do you apportion blame? When I see such an offence penalised I sometimes wonder how on earth the referee arrived at his decision – was it guesswork or really well-founded knowledge, or was it simply the fact that some 'overlord' or Referees' Society Godfather had said, 'Penalise the buggers and give the penalty to the side who had territorial disadvantage – there's unlikely to be a kick at goal but at least you'll stop their shenanagans.'

We can be far more convincing than that, and as a base for reasoning we have to start by assuming that the put-in team are not going to do something obviously foolish that would result in a penalty against them, particularly if up until that stage they have been able to win their fair share of the ball. Secondly, you have to consider where the scrummage is taking place: the nearer the goal line on an attacking put-in, the less likely it is that the attackers are going to infringe; the nearer the goal line on the defence's put-in, the greater the possibility. As the players also realise this, it is just possible that they might try to con the referee, particularly if the score is close or the scrum is near to the posts or time is fast running out, and because they think they understand the way the referee reacts to this type of situation the loose-head might just risk going down on his own put-in. Mind you, there will be one hell of a fuss as he tries to attract your attention to the so-called pressure, and his colleagues are not beyond joining in the act with offstage remarks like 'Hold him up, Joe, don't let him pull you down' as they try and con you into taking this wrong decision.

If you consider the mechanics, it is possible to make a reasonable deduction and not to be fooled. The tight-head is trying to bear down and the loose-head is trying to lift to a point where his hooker is fairly comfortable for the strike; both tight-head and loose-head will have straight backs, although they might be slightly angled and dipped before the ball is put in. Anything other than this denotes weakness and may well be your first sign when looking for the offender. However, assuming that all is equal and they are down, correctly positioned and bound and both applying the pressure their role requires, then you would be well advised to look at the legs of the loose-head prop. Just imagine yourself in his position, propping against, let's say, Graham Price: there is a lot of pressure, most of your effort is being sapped to neutralise this force and you suddenly make the decision to go down. Now, having been down before, there is no way you are going to hit the ground again with your head at a rate of knots, and you know that as soon as you give there is no way of applying the brake when you are halfway down. You know also that there is nothing the tight-head can do about this because by the time he realises the sudden change in pressure, it's too late, and probably his feet are so far back that he just can't take avoiding action. So you take the natural way out and as far as possible you lower yourself by going down onto your knees first, so reducing the impact of the head and neck and preventing the engine room pushing through and putting you in a position where you can cause injury to your neck. If the loose-head's head goes down directly onto the ground and his knees are not going down first, you can be sure that he is not responsible, because if he is responsible and he can do anything about it at all, he will go down first of all onto his knees to break that fall. That is something positive you can look for when you try to apportion blame for a collapsing scrum.

Ian McLauchlan, in *The Lions Speak*, claims that the tight-head is most responsible for the collapsing of the scrummage. He says that when the tight-head bores in, he tends to open up a gap which the other side can exploit, it weakens the firm grip that the front row have on each other and down they go. I'm not sure that I would agree; the part that matters is the junction of heads and shoulders and when a fellow is boring in, particularly if he has a longish arm, he can still make a tight unit and be open at the back. It is something which you can spot more clearly from on top than from anywhere else, but if that doesn't help and you suddenly see a hooker with a very red jaw after a quarter of an hour's play, it will give you a fair idea of what is going on. Look at the angled back of the tight-head and prevent him pushing in at that angle because not only is it dangerous, as suggested by Dr Silvers, it is the sort of thing, even if it is not done properly, that is going to irritate. If it does irritate, those fellows will try and do something about it and the game will become physical.

No matter which book you read about scrummaging, or which coach you talk to about its techniques, the words 'strength' and 'pressure' will be repeated time and again. If you have been unfortunate enough to experience the pressure yourself, you will know only too well the lengths to which players will go to avoid it. If you can appreciate that, and that front-row binding can also influence the height of scrummaging above the ground (that is to say the hooker's 'one arm over and one arm under' technique), then for the most part your decisions will be right, and certainly far more fair than those of any assessor who advocates what I call the phoney penalty.

Just think what is the most irritating part of scrummaging you experience when refereeing a match. Whatever your answer, be it unsettled movement prior to the put-in, crabbing, wheeling, collapsing, incorrect feed, fringe obstruction, it can almost always be traced back to the tunnel. Get the tunnel right and most of your troubles will be over before the second-phase irritation begins.

If you let the front rows scrummage close to the ground, it is difficult for the scrum-half to put the ball into the scrum from the position the law requires, holding it midway between the knee and ankle and a metre from the scrum. The heads of the props are in the way and he really does not have the tunnel that the law says he should have. So he either moves in closer to the scrum or holds the ball down at grass height. Meanwhile neither hooker can see the ball, so they are going to get a little irritated, and they are going to start causing that scrum to move about so that they get a better view. If they can't do it themselves within the law, they are going to get their props to bring pressure on the other side. Now it makes all the difference to a hooker's attitude in the centre of that front row if the ball is held correctly and he can see it – we have achieved a fair situation, where the ball can be contested fairly, and we have taken much of the aggravation out of the game.

Turning now to the scrum-half, according to the laws, he must keep his hands off his opponents when skirting the scrummage as he is following the ball round on his opponents' put-in. This is another commonsense situation which was never intended to be refereed to the letter of the law and providing that the scrum-half is not deliberately trying to cheat, play should continue. Put yourself in the scrum-half's position, skirting close to a scrum when the whole mass suddenly shifts; the natural thing for him to do is to stick out a hand to help him maintain a good, balanced position. There is a clear distinction between on the one hand this balancing action, and on the other a player who is involving himself in something more physical. If, however, the scrum-half steps inside the scrummage between the flanker and the no. 8, even though nothing physical is taking place, I wouldn't hesitate to penalise him because I believe that he has joined the scrummage from his opponents' side and so contravenes Law 24 (b) (1). This is an area where referees are inconsistent. It is a clear penalty offence which often goes unchecked, and it is quite likely to cause the kind of irritation that will result in blood-letting if you are not careful. Mind you, if it does go unchecked you can bet the players will find the answer, and it will not be long before the no. 8 unbinds with one hand and reaches across to bind on somewhere else and trap that scrum-half inside the scrummage. That is when it all starts to become physical.

As far as back-row play is concerned, one other offender who appears to be overlooked by referees is the flank forward who unbinds from a position in front of the ball and then breaks backwards into open play to make the extra man. You can see it happening in almost every International when an attacking side's scrummage is taking place close to their opponents' goal line or when the ball has been won by the defence who have then locked and are able to hold their opponents. The inconsistency in the handling of this offence suggests that many referees are sympathetic towards the move which is after all an attempt to promote open play. That might be the case, but referees cannot opt out of law and players at International level know what they can and cannot do.

The locks are the engine room in the second row. They are the chaps who are bound up on all sides, and they burn up so much energy that if they are doing their job properly they have neither the time nor the inclination to bugger about. However, if the temperature of the game is getting quite warm, keep your eye on their binding. They'll never be off-side, they are unlikely to cause the scrummage to collapse, nor can they interfere too much as far as fringe play is concerned, but they can and sometimes do settle the odd score by a left or right upper-cut which erupts from those subterranean passages. Be seen to be going through the motions as they form up, look at them closely and for longer than you would normally do, and you will find that it will have the desired effect.

Finally, can I quote what an assessor once said to me about the scrum when I was learning my trade: if it's untidy, in simple terms, blow it up and start again; and that isn't such a bad principle to start from. Try and keep the shape of the scrum clear and tidy, and don't let any player persist with lifting up and down, moving from side to side, holding the ball too low, putting the foot out, boring in at an angle, not binding properly. If the scrummage is clearly defined without wobbly edges and it has a hole in the middle, you have a chance. If it is moving and the edges are frayed and the hole is a blur, you are in trouble, because in those circumstances the players haven't a fair chance and the laws of the game were never designed to legislate unfairly against either side.

9

Coaching the Lineout

by BILL DICKINSON

*Bill Dickinson is Senior Lecturer at the Scottish
School of Physical Education, Jordanhill, Glasgow, where he has been a member of staff since
1948. A member of the Scottish Rugby Union's
Coaching Advisory Panel since its inception, he
acts as Director of the SRU's annual coaching
courses for club coaches. From 1971 to 1977 he
was adviser to the captain of the Scottish XV and
developed the scrummaging power of the Scottish front five.*

The great Dr Craven wrote in 1950 that the lineout was the
'illegitimate child of rugby football', and although the changes in
the laws since then have slightly improved that illegitimate
standard, I still have to produce in this chapter an illegitimate
child in a legitimate form.

The first priority in the lineout is that every player must know
the laws. He must not give away unnecessary penalty kicks
through not knowing the laws. He must know about the five-
metre line and he must know about the fifteen-metre line. He
must know about half-metre spacing, he must know about
one-metre spacing and he must know that if he is going to go
beyond the fifteen-metre line for a ball thrown overhead then he
must attempt to play that ball. He must know that if he joins the
lineout once it is formed, he cannot leave the lineout. So as a
coach you must instruct your players about the laws of the lineout
if they are not to concede unnecessary penalty kicks.

The next priority is organisation. We must have some codes
and not just throw the ball into the lineout haphazardly. Then we
must know where the ball is going, so there must be a skilled

thrower. Without the skill of throwing there is no lineout, there is a lottery. It has been conventional for the hooker, one of my favourite players, to throw the ball in because if he throws it from the left-hand touch line he'll throw it from the right-hand touch line and this makes for consistency. This is good but we must not dispense with other options. Occasionally, the wingers should throw – New Zealand have made good use of their wingers. I have even seen the scrum-half throw the ball in at every lineout, just as in seven-a-sides. Using the winger or scrum-half in this way means that you can have eight forwards in the line and the opposing winger has to be brought up close to the forwards to cover the front of the line. This both opens up the 'box' and makes it harder for that wing to cover should you decide to attack on the open side.

There are several types of throw. The lobbed ball is quite good if you are going to throw the ball over a lineout, especially a shortened lineout, when someone is going to run onto it. There is no value in doing any throw other than the torpedo throw, and it is not difficult. It has many advantages: it allows you to spin the ball, it allows you to throw it fast, it allows you to flight it, it also allows you to take a wide base and pretend to go for a long throw but throw soft. It gives deception, and part of lineout skill is deception. You need to use a ball of appropriate size, and some people like to steady the ball with the other hand. One word of caution: as the thrower follows through, the non-throwing shoulder very often falls, causing the ball to veer off-course. Keep the non-throwing shoulder up so that the ball will go down the intended line.

Who jumps? The easiest to develop is the aggressive, inward, upward jumper. Get a big guy who can do a bit of jumping and you can develop him. Remember that everybody must jump inwards: the law-makers have made it so by decreeing that the ball must come down in the middle. This means that in the lineout there will be contact. Usually the manufactured jumper is a no. 2 jumper. The other jumper needs a lot of innate ability. If you have a jumper who can go vertical without taking much of a pace forward or, better still, a jumper who can feint forwards, take his man slightly forwards and then take the ball going slightly backwards, develop his jumping spring to take advantage of this ability to use his body and beat his opponent. One of the best examples of this in recent years has been Alistair McHarg of Scotland: at Twickenham in 1977 Scotland were hammered by England, but England threw the ball into the line 32 times and

Alistair took 12 of their balls. Unfortunately Scotland did not do very much with the ball that was won, but McHarg had not only got jumping ability, he had the ability to deceive his opponent. The no. 4 jumper really needs this skill to make it difficult for his opposite number to know exactly what he is going to do.

Some jumpers at no. 4 step too far forward, and this was a problem when I was handling McHarg. They like to go forward and take the ball, especially when people are jumping in front of them, but this leaves a very big gap behind them which allows the opposition to come through. The only way you can block that gap is by stepping across, and usually this leads to a penalty kick because it is so blatant. So if you get a jumper like that, you have got to teach him to jump forward with the minimum amount of momentum to get lift, because if he takes too big a step he is making it very difficult. For example, during New Zealand's short tour of England and Scotland in 1979, Andy Haden was giving a public exhibition of lineout work everywhere he was going – one-handed catches, two-handed catches, the lot. I was asked to help to prepare the Glasgow side for the All Blacks match, and we made sure that Andy was not going to perform like that against us. He wasn't chosen because it was the International the next match, but someone was injured and Andy came on. What we did was to have one jumper jumping in front of him to bring him forward, New Zealand did not close the gap behind him, our boys poured through and their poor scrum-half got a hiding. It was very difficult for the New Zealanders to block that gap without giving a penalty kick and that is something which actually happened.

The ideal for which jumpers should aim is the two-handed catch, which can be accomplished if the timing, skill and jumping ability of the individual is greater than his opponent's; he can control the whole situation. Then there is the one-handed catch – getting up to the ball by elevating the shoulder – and I would always advocate using the dominant hand. We might want to make the not-so-good arm effective, but we must never make light of embellishing a talent. It means that on one touch line a player jumps with his inside hand, and on the other touch line he jumps with his outside hand. When the ball is caught it must be brought down, the body of the jumper must become an impregnable wall and the ball must be held out. If he is in difficulty others will help him, but the moment he makes contact he must have turned and be able to take any kind of shock pressure that is going to come onto him.

You can have a deflection by one or both hands, but I often wonder, when I see a jumper putting a two-handed deflection on it, why he couldn't have caught the ball. There may be occasions when it is better to put it into the scrum-half's hands than to catch the ball, but they are rare. The one-handed deflection is a real skill, the kind of skill shown by the water-polo player who can flick the ball down to wherever it is wanted.

Blocking causes all sorts of problems: tremendous difficulties for the referee, tremendous difficulties for the coach. The human eye can accommodate twelve-hundredths of a second's action. After that, you are dealing with impression. Look at the poor referee, trying to deal with five metres, fifteen metres, ten metres, the scrum-halves, the ball in the air, maybe six people from either side coming together. He has to judge the difference between illegal obstruction and legal blocking. The ball comes down a centre line and the players are on either side of that centre line. The jumper jumps inwards, so if you don't go for the jumper, he ends up in his opponent's line. His blocker behind must go forwards and inwards, his blocker in front must go forwards and inwards, otherwise they are going to be on the wrong side and there is no way round that. If there are any objections to that, then we have to go back to the law-makers and say to them, 'Why did you put people apart and let them jump in?' Whether we block going in behind or going in forwards is a matter of preference. If you have a jumper going forward whose high point is in front of him, and usually the most aggressive big guys will be able to use their power as well as their jumping skill there, it is usually easy for the rear man to go in backwards and form a wall and for the front man to go in forwards. If you want to drive, then both will have to go in the front, but why do you want to drive from lineout ball? You reduce twenty metres space to the same as scrummage spacing. The one time it might be worthwhile is when you are near the opponents' line and you want to have a surprise move.

There is a publication, which shall be nameless but it is very popular and sells well, which shows two blockers and a jumper, and it advocates the two blockers going across, joining arms behind the jumper. Now I have only ever seen that happen in a game twice, once when I played an International for the Blindness Island and once for the Girl Guides, because it is hellish difficult. Is a guy going to stand back and let you go round and get your arm there? I have never seen it work at good club level or at International level.

The front of the lineout can be profitable, but in Britain over the past few years it has been a disaster. Yet with a fast, low ball to an aggressive jumper, properly pulled down, it can be unbeatable possession. It's simple, but we've got to work at it.

The middle of the lineout usually means no. 4. It's very difficult. The ball to no. 4 has to be flighted a little bit because you usually find that no. 2 on the opposite side is either jumping or he has got his hands up and the trajectory has to be a little bit higher. It should be caught ball if possible, but sometimes it is desirable to deflect the ball into the scrum-half's hands and away.

The tail is really the glorious place. Why? Because the danger men to your backs are not really the opposite backs, it's nos. 6, 7 and 8 at the tail of their lineout. As soon as that ball is won those guys are off like a bomb. Those guys have got to be sucked in if you are going to use your backs, and by sending your ball to the tail of the lineout you ensure that those danger men, the opposing flankers and no. 8, are engaged in contesting the ball. Then, if you win the ball, they are certainly not in a position to go out and interfere and it is backs against backs. However, it is very difficult to be sure of getting the ball, although you can present difficulties to their nos. 6, 7 and 8 by massing your jumpers at the tail of the lineout. In my seven years with the Scottish national side I had jumpers of the calibre of the two Brown brothers and Alistair McHarg, and any International coach would have given his right arm to have three jumpers at one time. But I hadn't anybody to throw the ball past no. 6 with any degree of accuracy and so found it very difficult to utilise the skills of those players at the tail of the lineout.

Once you have won possession, attack not only by your backs but occasionally by your forwards. The lineout is not just a device for getting play started again, it is a platform for attack, and like any fighter you should go into the game not only with a good right hand but with a left jab that makes them stop and think for a moment. For example, when Scotland were in Paris in 1977, France played pretty miserably, with quite a lot of ball, and the French backs were not combining well at all. Scotland put a bit of pressure on France in the first ten minutes. Suddenly France changed the whole concept and started to roll the ball off the lineout, started to attack with the forwards. Scotland found it very difficult, although they scored three tries. To score three tries at Parc de Princes and not win is quite a devastating thought, but the French forwards changed the game and by attacking from lineout possession showed excellent tactical awareness.

There is only one attitude possible in defence in the lineout – win your opponents' ball. Mark the jumpers, that is the first thing. No. 2 in the line can jump or hold up his hand. If he starts to jump, then where is that ball going to go? It is certainly not going to no. 3. If it's going to no. 4, then it's going to go straight up and come down on him. You are going to dictate that that ball is likely to be at nos. 5, 6 or 7, and if you have some knowledge of where the ball is going to go then you have a better chance of attacking your opponents' throw.

What about no. 8 and no. 7, at the tail of your lineout? Some people say that the no. 8 should watch the scrum-half and then go out onto the fly-half, but I don't think that is reasonable at a high level of rugby. He must be off like a bomb and pressurise the fly-half into being a mere server of the ball, and if the opposition full-back is going to be a running full-back, then that will allow your fly-half to drift and allow you to play the drift defence. The no. 7 must then watch for the scrum-half dummying and coming round the tail of the lineout. The hooker, or the thrower, is the king of the five-metre line. If one of those piranha fish is waiting on the edge to sneak round he'll come in, bind over the top of him and that's him finished for the moment.

In covering the ball from the lineout, tell your players to get between the ball-carrier and their own line. If they are behind the ball-carrier, they will certainly be able to tell you the number of the player who scored because they will get a good view of his back, but they won't be close enough to make the tackle. In poor weather, they should pour through the gaps like a great avalanche and see how the scrum-half responds. It doesn't matter whether he is big or small, his heart will have to be very large to stand up to it.

Now the short lineout. First ask yourself, why the shortened lineout? Is it because you have two good jumpers and you can stop them being molested if it is just a straight jump, or do you have a shortened line so that you can move the ball out to some of the forwards who can drive forward, set up a maul, a second phase with an open side and a blind side because perhaps you haven't been terribly successful on the open side? A maul in-field gives you perhaps twenty metres to operate in. I didn't sleep some Friday nights, wondering what Pierre Villepreux would do going down the blind side when France would be peeling into the tail of the Scottish line and opening up a ten-metre gap for him. How much more could he have done if he had gone down a twenty-metre gap! The same applies to Andy Irvine, JPR or any other running full-back.

Finally, let me summarise the practical ingredients that any lineout coaching session should include:

1. Organisation of lineout calls and codes. It is essential that any team is equipped with its own codes of lineout signals. These signals should be known by every member of the team.
2. The technique of the maul.
3. Throwing in accurately to a single line of players with emphasis on:

   (a) The ball must be thrown down the middle
   (b) The catcher must make an effort to get in the air
   (c) The catcher must learn to turn his body in the air
   (d) The catcher must learn to bring the ball down quickly.

1, 2 and 3 must be practised and practised as they form the whole essence of lineout play.

4. The next stage is to bring two lines together and develop as follows:

   (a) One team jumps as in 1, 2 and 3 above. Their opponents are at this time passive.
   (b) As in (a) above, except that on a given signal the opposition are going to go through the gaps.
   (c) The position of the throw is not varied at this stage but continually thrown to no. 2.
   (d) The tactical part to know is that the last man must not commit himself. He must make his immediate opponent go around him in order to tackle the fly-half.

5. Blocking must be taught. The blockers either side of the jumper must learn to bind in on the jumper *after* he has jumped, turned and returned to the ground. The essential quality of the blocker in this situation is *speed*.
6. Practise the above techniques until effective, then vary the position of the throw and the catcher. NB: Always react to the situation, for example, if a loose ball occurs it must be tidied up.
7. Practise other variations:

   (a) Long ball to the last man
   (b) The peel

(c)   The no. 4 to knocking down to no. 2 and attack around the front.

(d)   Three-man lineout; stretch the line; compress the line; use all the space available by moving backwards and forwards to receive the ball.

8   Bring in the threequarters and practise lineout with forwards and moving the ball to the backs.

9   Bring in full opposition and practise match situations from lineout.

10   The game situation should be developed and faults or improper techniques such as blocking spotted, isolated and corrected and put back into a game situation.

The most important thing about the training field is this – attitude. If we do not train seriously, if you do not put reasonable pressure upon your players to make them give of their best, the only thing they can transfer from the training field is a lax attitude. You cannot train casually and suddenly play seriously, so be nice, but be insistent.

10

Refereeing the Lineout

by JOHN PRING

John Pring is one of the leading New Zealand referees since the war, and had charge of all four Tests of the 1971 Lions series. He is a past president and life member of the Auckland Referees' Association and has been an active official for 33 years following an injury that curtailed his playing career.

This chapter is called 'Refereeing the Lineout', but a better title would be 'The Lineout and its Trouble Spots'. It will not become too technical, because there is no answer to those trouble spots except through referees themselves, with the co-operation of the players to play within the laws.

Law 23 is called 'Touch and Lineout'. It takes up six pages, with two pages of instruction and notes, not to forget each country's casebook of law, which in New Zealand consists of six pages. This all makes for a very comprehensive law, an involved, technical listing of do's and don'ts. Considering that it is only a way of re-starting the game, one often wonders if the lineout is worth all the words which are written about it. It is certainly the biggest and most involved law of the game, but it is also an integral part of the game, and we could lose something special to rugby if we were to alter it from the way it is. Compared with other methods, it is by far the fairest way of re-starting play as long as the laws are observed.

Accepting the fact that this is the way the game is to be played, the referee has the mammoth task of adjudicating comprehensive law with so many diverse situations able to arise. He is responsible for seeing that the lineout is fairly and correctly played, and he must be firm and consistent in his decisions. In any game his knowledge of the law should be above question and his concentration must be 100%, but above all he should be aware of what the teams are trying to achieve. For example, is their objective to gain the direct feed of the ball, or are they trying the peel-off movement, or perhaps the drive from the front of the lineout? These are the things a referee has got to be thinking about. Players know their drill, they have trained for it, so the least the referee can do is to understand their skill.

Any referee with no feeling or understanding of the game, who did not understand the motives of the players, could penalise every lineout for some form of technicality; there are over thirty offences for which penalties could be awarded. But naturally this would be bad for the game, so we expect all players to respect fair play and the referee through his knowledge of the objects and methods of players to allow the game to flow for the enjoyment of all participants. A referee must be positive in his thinking and in his use of the law of advantage, which can be applied to all phases of the lineout. This is where we impose our different personalities, and our application of advantage determines our ability to handle this important part of the game. Many coaches and players are lazy, the technicalities of the law are a bore to them, and they make little effort to master it completely. They are more likely to play to the referee of the day and learn the hard way from the whistle that some particular play is not on today.

In discussing or thinking about the lineout, I like to divide it into four segments of formation and play:

Phase 1 The ball going into touch
Phase 2 The formation of the lineout
Phase 3 The beginning of a lineout until the ball touches a player or the ground
Phase 4 From when the ball lands along the line of touch until the lineout has ended.

Phase 1. I don't intend to dwell on this as it is straightforward and causes few problems, other than pointing out to touch judges that when the ball in flight swings out over the touch line and comes back into the field of play, it is a terrible temptation to raise your flag prematurely just to see the wind swirl the ball back into play; this has left many touch judges with red faces.

Phase 2. The formation of the lineout is when you should be first to the spot. Unless there is a quick throw-in, it is a time when you can gather your thoughts. It is certainly not a time to relax and think of the errors you have already made, you must forget about what has been and think ahead. Where's the ball? Has it been retrieved by a player? Where are the five- and fifteen-metre marks? Have the non-participating players retired ten metres from the line of touch? How about the participating players and their spacing, and that very important half-metre gap between the two teams? It is a very important time for thinking and concentration. Also, you should be giving thought to your position at the lineout. You will have listened to the teams' conversations as they approach the lineout, you will have noted who is attacking and who is defending, and you will take up your position in what you think is the most effective spot for that particular lineout. It will be a position where you can effectively observe and anticipate the next flow of play. The formation of the lineout is not a time to relax: be the first there, without making a big show of it. Then sit and watch the players coming up – it will boost your confidence, if you don't feel particularly fit, to watch the players puffing and panting back to the spot, and it gives them confidence to think that you are already there.

Phase 3. The beginning of the lineout, from the time the ball leaves the hands of the thrower until it touches the ground or is touched by another player, is just a second or two, but it is the most crucial phase of the lineout from a referee's point of view. It is a period when only a few players should be participating actively, only those who are jumping for the ball or peeling off. This is the stage when a referee must be firm in his decisions because everything that is going to happen is going to start in this most crucial period. This is where players play up to and beyond the law if the referee of the day will allow. The harmony of a game can be destroyed if the referee does not observe the blatant illegalities which commence at this phase. It is a time when players will lose confidence in your ability and will take unfortunate remedial action to rectify an obstruction which you should have noticed. There are four main points to watch during this phase:

(a)   The player who leaves the lineout prematurely as if for a peeling-off movement, as he is quite entitled to do as soon as the ball has left the thrower's hand. But he must keep moving if he is participating in a genuine peeling-off movement, or he must remain in the lineout until the ball has

95

touched a player or the ground. How often have we seen, let's say, a no. 5 in the lineout expertly catching the ball but immediately on his landing being driven backwards by three or four of the opposition. How could they all have possibly arrived at that moment without leaving the lineout prematurely? The player who is catching that ball must be given a chance to do so without being jostled and pushed, and a chance to prepare what he is going to do with the ball when he has caught it. Those few seconds are vital, and the players cannot peel off prematurely simply for the purpose of the drive. The peeling-off law is a good law when played and refereed correctly. The great problem is provided by the players who illegally peel off the lineout when the ball leaves the hands of the player throwing it in, and who intentionally loiter in the vicinity of where the ball is to land. The referee thinks they are leaving the lineout for the peeling-off movement and then he gets distracted by something else and before he knows it the ball has landed and everything is happening. He has lost sight of those players who have peeled off and it is not for maybe that lineout or the next one that he suddenly realises what they are doing. Then he must watch them much closer at the next lineout. Never rule on what you don't know has happened. You are only suspicious of what has happened so you can't rule on it, but at the next lineout pay more attention to that particular point.

(b) The player who is supposed to be jumping for the ball but instead throws his whole body across his opposite number, obstructing as he does so, upsetting the lineout, upsetting everybody by throwing himself diagonally across in most cases, and more often than not landing in an off-side position. Such players are given far too much latitude and when in the off-side position don't seem to realise that they must make some attempt to retire and should certainly not interfere with play while in that position.

(c) That half-metre gap down the line of touch, especially at the end of the lineout where so much holding and obstruction occurs. Watch especially for the opposing player who steps into the opposite side of the lineout before the ball lands, enabling him to gain that extra half-metre when the lineout ends. Nos. 7 and 8 in the lineout are a touchy and inflammable breed of player, as they are the fast boys and are usually impatient to dive out and harass the scrum-half and the fly-half. At the end of the lineout, the lines of players tend to crowd in together in their efforts to sight the player throwing in the ball, so insist on the gap being maintained and let them know right from the start that the less contact they have with each other, the less irritation there will be and the better for the game.

(d) The player who jumps and taps the ball with one hand. Be suspicious of him, especially if he gains great height. What is he doing with the other hand? How did he get so high? Is he pushing the opposition? Pay more attention to him at the next lineout and let it be known right from the start that that sort of play is not on.

Phase 4. This is the phase from when the ball lands or is touched until the lineout ends. Unless the ball is tapped or deflected, this phase of the lineout can be a shambles, but only if the referee has not taken the correct action at phase 3. It is here, when the ball is bouncing around and no-one can grasp it, that players who have got themselves into an off-side position so often participate in play. Here again, be strong, take firm action right from the start on illegalities, and the tidiness of the lineout will improve almost immediately. Another weakness which occurs in our control during this phase is the non-participating players advancing from the ten-metre line before the lineout has ended. This is particularly noticeable when the lineout ruck or maul is still taking place on the line of touch. Now it must be very difficult for the player to decide when the lineout has ended, and his decision to advance may not coincide with the opinion of the referee, so it is in some cases a very tricky decision for the player, especially when it is in front of his own goal posts. We can be sympathetic, but only the referee can be right – as the law very clearly shows, he is the sole judge! As a suggestion to help in this very grey area of play, perhaps we could assist the game by introducing a signal to indicate that the lineout has ended. Then there would be no excuse for the players to advance prematurely.

Now a little bit about the short lineout. This type of lineout is being used more and more and requires much quicker thinking and action on the part of the referee. He must be instantly alert about the requirements of the law, and he must position himself for an overall view of participating and non-participating players. So much depends on various points, such as when the lineout begins, whether it is a long throw-in, and when the lineout finishes. I don't think that it would be unfair to say that the forwards who have had to retire to the ten-metre line have very little idea of when the lineout ends, or that they cannot advance for the long throw-in unless the backs of the team throwing in the ball advance first, and that the ball must go beyond the furthest player. That is why we have to be alert for the short lineout: so much happens in law in such a very short time.

Whatever we do, we must all be consistent in our application of the laws, right from the first lineout. To be fair to players and our fellow-referees we must all be consistent in every game; I am always a little suspicious about the so-called 'popular' referee, and when I hear players talking about the popular referee I wonder about the things he hasn't been refereeing properly and where he has been letting other referees down.

Application of the law in the lineout is a skill which some of us have to a greater extent than others. No-one can write down that you must referee this way or that way; it becomes a very personal thing in its application, and the skill of application is usually the difference between an average referee and a good referee. We all know that we could penalise at every lineout for some kind of technicality, and that it is our skill which can help to make a good lineout, but any foul play or misconduct must be dealt with immediately.

In drawing attention to the trouble spots in the lineout, I cannot guarantee how we can have an incident-free lineout while we have players contesting possession from the throw-in from touch but, by understanding the intentions of the law, by recognising the moves of the players, by distinguishing between the player who deliberately breaks the law and the player who unintentionally plays beyond the law, by being severe in eliminating foul play and by consistent and correct application of the laws in conjunction with advantage, you can win the players' confidence in your ability and control the flow of the ball without the irritation of constant stoppages.

11

Coaching the Ruck

by BILL FREEMAN

Bill Freeman is Director of Coaching to the New Zealand Rugby Union, following a long career in the game as player, administrator and provincial coach. A Wellington man, he played at first five-eighth for his province. On retirement he served as a club and provincial administrator before becoming a member of the NZRU Executive and its Council.

This chapter deals with one aspect of the game which we recognise as the ruck, but rugby is divided into many aspects about which we are all continually learning as much as we possibly can. Coaches must be ever aware of the danger of accepting any one aspect as the whole, and to be a successful coach you must ensure that you do not become orientated by that part of the game which was your particular strength as a player, thus creating performance which only expresses that part of the game. It is a jigsaw, and you must be prepared to extend your knowledge by learning other aspects in depth.

Turning now to the ruck, it is a very important part of the game in New Zealand. Its importance is clearly because of its simplicity: we have 200,000 players and 10,000 coaches and they are all in essence simple guys. Because of our emphasis on simplicity we have a saying which is known as the K.I.S.S. This is used by the players when the coach gets very smart and very clever, and is asked by the players to 'Keep It Simple, Stupid!'

Initially we must consider the approach to the ruck. The principle which motivates New Zealand to consider rucking as such an important aspect of play is that in general players are always going forward when rucking, and when mauling they are usually going backwards. The basis for rucking successfully is therefore formation, and the winning of ball with your body. Many coaches believe that rucking means using the boot, but we do not use the boot in New Zealand; in fact, if you were able to get close enough to a New Zealand pack as it went beyond the ball, smashing the opposition backwards, you would hear them saying, 'Excuse me, excuse me!' There are many tensions and lots of body action in our game which when controlled are both skilled and very exciting, and the ruck is one example.

No pack of forwards can become dominant unless it understands that it must be well organised in what it is preparing to do. All who participate in the ruck must understand the key factors, which are: bend, bind, drive and link as early as possible with the appropriate supporting player. Players must also understand their positional responsibilities about the field. In the ruck the positional responsibilities are extremely important, and we must understand that its structure is based on seven ball-getters in a 2-3-2 formation and one player standing off to create where necessary continuity of forward possession. In essence it is the power of the unit to win the ball without a conventional hooker. Provided each player knows his positional duties as he arrives at the ruck, and to bend, bind and drive beyond the ball, the structure will produce possession. A flanker who arrives at the ruck must become a hooker, get his head in and produce the necessary positional skill and dynamics of the ball-winner. In exactly the same way, the hooker arriving last must keep his head out and accept the responsibilities of the supporter.

The coach must have decided his objective and planned a way to achieve it. With the ruck, he must first consider when and how he wishes to gain possession for the use of this technique. Is it by diving on the ball and placing it in an advantageous position, or perhaps by engaging the opposition over the ball and folding them backwards? There are many ways in which we can set up the ruck, and a good coach must give his players the practical options they will experience in the game.

A ruck is not automatic because the ball happens to be on the ground. It can be picked up and carried forward. If the opposition then engages the player carrying the ball, he can remain in a forward-facing position and with correct positional skills form the structure of the ruck. Where the opposition arrives before your ruck then you must get lower than them and with positional and structural skills fold them back beyond the ball. The final, but extremely important, facet of rucking is the speed at which the structure 2-3-2 is established. This affects the dynamics of the ruck. Players must decide where they will join the ruck as they make their approach run, ensuring that they join in a supporting position which keeps the ruck in line and avoids any spin or wheel. Having made that decision, they should shorten and quicken their stride to ensure that the dynamics of the ruck force the opposition beyond the ball.

The key factors associated with good rucking are summarised in the following simple terms:

STRUCTURE

The simplicity of the supporting player's role.

Bending, binding, driving, preferably with another player; the torso bent forward from the hips, head up, back straight, shoulders hunched.

The grip, as in the scrummage, strong and secure.

Where possible, drive to leave the ball for the scrum-half.

Where necessary, the eighth forward plays the standing-off support role.

Go beyond the ball, keeping yourself and the opposition on their feet.

Keep your eyes open.

Come in low and drive up, keeping your balance, with your spine in line with the direction in which the ruck should be moving.

Be dynamic, using a short leg-drive.

POSSESSION

When play has broken down, possession may be gained in a number of ways, using the ruck as an effective means of re-creating continuity. These possession options are easily understood by players and simple to coach.

The most common manner in which possession is gained is by a player diving on the loose ball and placing it advantageously for his team. Other methods include:

Picking up and angling into the opposition and, whilst the supporting drive is on, squeezing the ball to the ground.

By presenting an opposition forward with the ball for squeezing to the ground on a supporting forward drive.

By driving loosely-knit opposition forwards back beyond the ball.

SKILL BUILDING

Skill building is essential if the ruck is to be a well-drilled, dynamic aspect of play, which leads on to the all-important practical appreciation which is what gives players and coaches enjoyment and is why they are involved in the game. As with any other aspect of play, preparation is essential. Repetition with variation is the balance required for an enjoyable and effective practice session. In the next paragraphs I try to create some balance of practical suggestions for coaching ruck. Depending upon the group of players concerned not every exercise may be necessary; for example the initial exercise will be for players who are not practised in the skills of rucking. Although in the figures accompanying the exercises the players are wearing the numbers on their backs which they might expect to wear in a game, in the text, the numbers refer to the order in which the players arrive at the ruck.

Exercise 1   Skill building
One pushing on one laterally and up and down.
Two on two as above.
Two plus one on two plus one as above.
Individuals running to dive on the ball.
Add two players, building the foundation.
Add three players for drive.

Exercise 2   Unopposed approach and set-up (2–3 system)
Initially without opposition, other than for the purposes of support, two players place themselves not too far beyond the ball, which is lying on the ground, at the same time ensuring the positional and structural skills which would resist being folded backwards by the initial opposition attack. The first-line attack of two players is then supported from behind by three more players who carefully choose their approach to avoid spinning and wheeling the ruck foundation, and who at the same time create power through dynamics to the prime attack. This is the 2–3 set-up and is the primary point for coaching correction. See Figs. 15 and 15a. At this stage the coach must be looking for all the structural skills, i.e. come in low, bend, bind, drive, positional

Fig. 15

Fig. 15a

responsibilities. This exercise is repeated until the approach and initial foundation of the five participants is satisfactory. Key factors:

i   Ball on ground.
ii   Players 1 and 2 who bind together beyond the ball.
iii   Player 3 positions and binds between 1 and 2.
iv   Players 4 and 5 bind and drive on either side for an on-line attack.
v   None of the players risk playing the ball with their feet, ensuring it is won by driving past it.
vi   Initial possession is ignored at this stage to build the correct foundation.
vii   Foot and body positions for dynamics.

Exercise 3   Unopposed approach and set-up (2-3-2)
Using the same principles as we did in exercise 2, we now progress to the use of the seven forwards (Figs. 16 and 16a). Key factors:

Fig. 16

Fig. 16a

i–vii   As in exercise 2.
 viii   Greater emphasis on binding together by players 4 and 5,
        and 6 and 7.
   ix   Positional play must be examined to avoid spin or wheel
        and to ensure driving is in line.

Exercise 4   Gaining possession
In this exercise we take into consideration gaining possession,
that is we condition the practice to encompass the initial possession of the ball from loose play by introducing an eighth forward
who will be nominated by the captain or pack-leader to dive on
the ball and place it in an advantageous position for his supporting forwards (Fig. 17). Having released the ball to the position of
advantage, he will cover up to avoid coming into contact with the
boots of his supporting fowards. The other forwards will form the
foundation (Figs. 17a–d). Look for organisation by the leader,
players' positional skills, their dynamics, the drive in line, leaving
the ball where it was placed by player no. 1. The coach must be
circling to check and correct errors instantly. Slow down the
approach. Key factors:

105

Fig. 17

Fig. 17a

Fig. 17b

Fig. 17c

Fig. 17d

i–ix   As in exercise 3.
  x   Players arriving in positions 2 and 3 must get their front leg
      over player 1 but remain in a strong enough position to
      resist being folded back by opponents, and not touch the
      ball.

Exercise 5   Improving positional skills and dynamics
In this exercise the aim is to improve the overall skill of rucking
by putting the technique the players have developed in the
previous exercises under the pressure of conditioned opposition
from other players in a seven against five situation, ie. 2-3-2
versus 3-2. Key factors:

i–x   As in exercise 4.
  xi   The analysis of individual faults to create skill and commit-
       ment.

Exercise 6   Loose ball after a tackle
Eight players start in scrum formation against the scrum
machine. At several positions on the field of play a tackle bag is

placed on its end with a ball balanced on the top of each bag. A player breaks from the scrum and tackles the first bag. The ball falls to the ground and is dived on by a second player who places it in a position of advantage. The ruck is formed and if the coach is satisfied, the forwards progress to the next position. The exercise is repeated until all tackles have been made. Then they run back to machine.

Exercise 7   Player picks up loose ball and drives into opposition
In this exercise the loose ball is picked up by a nominated player, no. 1, who drives into two players holding a tackle bag (Fig. 18). At the same time, he angles his shoulder and hip towards the tackle bag and places the ball against the other hip. He is quickly supported by players 2 and 3, who drive either side and beyond the ball, folding back the players holding the tackle bag (Fig. 18a). Players 4 and 5 drive between 2 and 3 and players 6 and 7 position themselves either side of 4 and 5 (Fig. 18b). Player 8 drives between 4 and 5 (Fig. 18c). When the player carrying the ball feels the drive, he squeezes the ball to the ground and all fowards walk over the ball. Ideally, the ball-carrier must keep possession and position until the drive is achieved. However, if he feels he cannot, then he can force himself to the ground, placing the ball in a position where it can be played back by the feet of his support players.

Exercise 8   Variation when player drives into opposition
As in exercise 7 the ball is picked up by a player (no. 1), who drives into opposition in the form of two players in a position to make a standing tackle (Fig. 19). The ball-carrier points one shoulder and hip, holding the ball tight against the opposite hip. He is then supported by the next player (no. 2), who drives beyond the ball into the opposition, at the same time binding with the ball-carrier. The next supporing players, 3, 4 and 5, bind in behind the first two players and two more players, 6 and 7, bend and drive between 3, 4 and 5 (Fig. 19b). This leaves player 8 clear to support by continuing the forward drive or distributing his backs (Fig. 19c). This can lead to forwards running at backs and creating overlaps. Key factors:

i–xi As in exercise 5.
xii Protection of the ball whilst off the ground.
xiii Smashing, driving attack by player 2, the first support forward.

Fig. 18

Fig. 18a

Fig. 18b

Fig. 18c

Fig. 19

Fig. 19a

Fig. 19b

Fig. 19c

xiv   Variation of number of holding players to produce greater drive from attack.

xv   Work on shortening the time taken to complete the ruck foundation.

Finally, I must emphasise the importance of variation when coaching the ruck foundation and set-up. Greater variation on the theme is achievable than space has allowed here. Obviously variation and the introduction of opposition creates greater interest and enjoyment for players. Backs as well as forwards should be used in the development of the ruck as part of the team tactics, remembering to build the session in simple stages, initially unopposed. When you and your players are satisfied with the technique, then the opposition can be introduced in a conditioned game to improve skills. At this stage do not be satisfied to observe from a distance, but try to be as close to each stage of the build-up as possible, conversing with individuals and the leader as and when correction is needed. This helps your overall assessment at the final stage.

In New Zealand, rucking is the dominant skill in second-phase play because it is very dynamic and gives backs as well as forwards far more attacking options, the simplest being orthodox delivery to the winger which stretches the opposition. However, it should not detract from the practice of picking up the loose ball and going foward whilst inter-passing. It is only when this phase of the game is impracticable or breaks down that we need to ruck to re-create continuity, and unlike mauling, the build-up, foundation and set-up is carried out with continued momentum. In the future, more consideration will have to be given to rucking because organised defence will make it more and more difficult for teams to use possession from set pieces effectively. Finally, remember to give your practice session the K.I.S.S. of life – Keep It Simple, Stupid!

12

Coaching the Maul

by SYD MILLAR

One of the outstanding figures of the modern game as player, coach and manager, Syd Millar was capped 37 times for Ireland and made three Lions tours in 1959, 1962 and 1968, appearing in nine Tests. He first coached Ulster, then Ireland while also serving as a selector, before coaching the successful and unbeaten 1974 Lions. He remained an important figure in Irish and British rugby, and managed the 1980 Lions.

One cannot isolate parts of rugby football from the whole game, so we must look at the maul in the context of rugby football as a game of 'stretching' the opposition and 'driving' at them. Recently, we in the UK and Ireland have over-emphasised the driving to the detriment of the stretching. Our game is out of balance and generally we tend to be driving more and stretching much less than we should. The reason for this can be seen if you look at Lions' performances in the recent past. When we played New Zealand or South Africa, we expected to survive and possibly win with maybe 35% or 40% of the ball. We had to have backs who used what ball they received well. We also tended to have quicker and lighter flank forwards. In the late 1960s we put more emphasis on forward play, where we were so deficient, and the one area that was perhaps easiest to put right was the scrum. We therefore emphasised the scrum, which was right and proper and did bear fruit, but we moved too far towards forward play. What has this to do with the maul? If you develop your forward play and particularly your scrum, you will find your mauling will also improve because there are more mauls following scrums than there are following lineouts. So with the development of our scrummaging techniques, mauling became a bigger and bigger part of our game. If you have a good scrum platform, your back row and half-backs can use the ball. If the back row drives from a scrum and a maul is set up, we have to become good at mauling to use this platform. This became self-generating, and we found we had another maul followed by another maul. The maul is still an important part of our game, but we have perhaps overdone the holding and retaining of the ball by the forwards.

In the last chapter, Bill Freeman stated, 'You ruck going fowards, and you maul going backwards.' There is a lot of truth in this generalisation. If the ball is put behind you, in order for your defence to re-group you want to slow the game down. In this case the maul is probably a better option than the ruck because it is slower and you maintain control of the ball. Unfortunately, the opposite happens too often in our rugby and we get maul ball going foward leading to the situation of maul, maul, maul. Ask any back how he wants the ball and he will probably tell you: either when the pack are going forward, or quickly. At times we have forgotten those principles, and in situations where they should give the ball quickly, the pack retains it and rolls it off to maul again. There are times when this is the correct option but we tend to overdo it. If you over-emphasise one aspect of play, you not only change the pattern of play, you also change the type of player you produce. If you look at the situation in Britain at present and think of quick flankers, there aren't many about. One of the reasons for this is the change in our play. I would certainly like to see us get back to the situation where we produce quicker ball from the maul and perhaps use the ruck a bit more.

It is most important that coaches tell players not only how to do things but also why they are doing them. When one talks about the maul in relation to the whole game, players sometimes fail to realise that the ball may come back quickly or be driven. The maul is an area where the coach may do a lot of work, but when the team goes on the field, because of a lack of appreciation of the game they don't do the right thing. The aim of the coach is to make himself obsolete, in that the players know as much as or more than he does. The coach is someone who has experience and can communicate to the players so that they go out and use tactics which they themselves recognise as necessary in a particular situation.

There are two types of maul. First, the static maul, for example at the kick-off where your forwards field the ball and all they can do is catch it, set up the maul and deliver it for a kick, or perhaps attempt to roll it off. It does not lead to much because it is very like the set scrum where the defence is aligned and you haven't really disturbed the opposition's defensive pattern at all. The second type, the dynamic maul, is where things really start to happen. It is dynamic in that it is going foward and the opposition are involved. Perhaps it comes from a player running off the side of a static maul and creating another one, or a dynamic maul might be produced from a set piece, so that the opposition have to come back and re-group, or some of their defensive players are involved.

Mauls happen without us deliberately creating them, but we can also create them. If, for example, we have a good scrum platform, we can use our back row or backs to create situations where we involve the opposition back row, or perhaps even some of their backs. If my pack is much stronger than the opposition, then I certainly want to use their strength against the opposition's weakness. One way of doing this is to have a good scrum platform, and using the ball won to drive at the lighter opposition. It is done deliberately to vary play, to cause more problems for the other side or to prevent opposing players putting pressure on my half-backs.

In the maul the player in possession, setting up the maul, must stay on his feet. This is a skill in itself and is very important. The first man in support takes the ball from him and the rest of the forwards build up the maul around him. Support has to be there quickly. It is also important that the support players bend their bodies and hit the maul with their shoulders if they are going to drive it, or support the people who are there first. If the maul is static and we want to inject some movement into it, then forwards arriving and hitting the maul properly, with their bodies bent and using their shoulders to drive, will inject that movement. Too often players arrive at the maul, they stop, they bend, the whole thing falls down and we have the pile-up that is so prevalent. Body angle is very important.

Don't turn your back as you go into a man. If you do, he can shift you over. That's a weak way to drive, whereas if you use your shoulder it's much harder for him. Bend your body, leave the ball on your hip and dip the shoulder. As well as the support player, the ball-carrier has a contribution to make to the maul, and that is to use his shoulder, not his gut.

Another factor in dealing with the maul is decision. A decision has to be made when to give the ball and what to do with it, and this is where game appreciation comes in. So often we take the easy option and set up another maul without achieving very much from it. So a decision has to be made by the ball-holder, whether he gives it quickly or retains it. If I were a back today I would be a bit worried about this aspect of decision-making as too often the decision is to retain possession by rolling it around the side and driving it a bit further.

One key principle of rugby football is to go foward. If a scrum, a ruck, a maul or a back-row move does not go forward, then the opposition have no problems in defence. On the other hand, if you can cross the gain line and drive over it, with quick ball coming back it is far more difficult to defend.

Whilst forwards are more involved in this aspect of the game than backs, everybody must be able to maul. Everyone must be aware of the ball-carrier requiring help, so not only forwards but also backs must be prepared to go in and support him. Securing

Fig. 20

the ball is so important that the second man there, whether he be a back or a forward, must go and help to retain possession of the ball.

Turning now to practical work, warm up by asking four players to jog across the field (never up and down). Two of them go in front and are driven into by the ball-carrier. The fourth man supports the ball-carrier and rips the ball out. It's all very simple, but teaches close support.

For the next exercise (Fig. 20), again using the whole pitch right across, put all the forwards except two in a single line. The ball-carrier drives into the first man, the support player takes the ball and drives into the next man in line. The original ball-carrier is now the support player, drives into the third man, and so on. This emphasises the need for the body to be bent and for close support.

The next exercise is similar, but as each player is driven into, he becomes an additional support player (Fig. 21), and a full-scale maul is set up on the last man (Figs. 21a and 21b). Again, try and develop close support, look at the body angle and the use of the shoulder.

Next, four players including the ball-carrier face three other players. They drive in, with the first support player taking the ball and the other two binding over. They drive forward, and the ball is fed back. The feed must be quick. Often we see the first support player take the ball, he stands there and passes it on, the next guy takes it, stands there, give it to the next guy, and so on back to the scrum-half who can do little with it. So the best mauls are where we drive, drive, drive until it's the right time to give it.

If we drive but it becomes a static maul, we can either practise leaving someone out to receive the ball from the scrum-half and drive on the short side or the open side, or we can roll off it, especially if most of our players are in there and we have nobody free to drive off. Or, of course, we can feed our backs. The trap to avoid is using a static maul to create another static maul, which is a danger if you are too adamant about rucking going forward and mauling going back; that's taking the decision away from your players in any game situation. Going forward, it is fine to put the ball on the ground, go over it and it's there for the half-back, but often it is much better if the forwards control the ball in their hands, that they make the decision to give it or to drive it or to roll it off. Of course, if the ball is behind most of the players, they have got to get it back. That's where we want to make it a static maul, to give time for our players to re-group in defence or

119

present the ball to the scrum-half to kick it, for in that situation it's not often we can counterattack at all.

Arms are important in rugby football, especially for the forwards. They have to scrum with them, bind with them, use them in mauls. But ripping the ball out of a maul demands the use of the body as well, and a good practical exercise is in twos, one man clutching the ball to his stomach while the other wedges his arm between the ball and the carrier's stomach, ripping downwards with the weight of his body behind his shoulder.

Once you have got the physical things right, get your forwards to understand what they are doing and why they are doing it, and the difficulties that thay pose for the backs if they produce slow ball for them; probably the only options the backs have left are to kick or to try and create a maul or ruck in the middle of the field

Fig. 21

Fig. 21a

Fig. 21b

without much chance of crossing the gain line. So good mauling forwards appreciate when to give the backs the ball and when to drive it on. If I was a scrum-half, I would want the ball while my backs were coming up because the opposition backs have maybe got to step back. It becomes like a set scrum if my backs are static, and wastes the opportunities for attack provided by good second-phase ball.

If the maul is used for good tactical reasons – to involve the opposition back row from a set scrum, to take on a lighter opposition pack physically – fine, but the cardinal thing to work on is good ball, that is ball going forward, or ball given quickly. The other points about body angle and about close support are of course worthwhile, but when to stretch and when to drive – that's really what rugby is about.

13

Refereeing the Tackle Law, Ruck and Maul

by CLIVE NORLING

A member of the WRU's International Panel, Clive Norling sustained a back injury when playing for Neath Grammar School in 1969 and became a referee to join the RFU's list when a student at Portsmouth Polytechnic. He returned to Wales in 1974 and was placed on the WRU list, becoming a member of the Panel in 1977. He is secretary of the Welsh Referees' Laws Committee and is extremely interested in the development of the game as a coach.

The pile-up is one of the least attractive features of the game of rugby, but I don't really like to use the word pile-up because it suggests that there is something there that isn't really covered in law at all. If you referee correctly Law 18 (the tackle law) and Law 19 (the law dealing with a player lying with, near or on the ball) and the players respond correctly to it, then we've got two further laws to cover players getting together after a tackle, that's the ruck and maul law, Law 21 and Law 22.

There are still too many referees opting out of refereeing the pile-up, myself included. Two seasons ago, when a side on its Easter tour was playing a side from Gwent, there was an almighty pile-up underneath the posts with the two visiting centres trapped at the bottom. It must have taken all of thirty seconds for the ball to come out, but it eventually rolled back and of course, the home side fly-half had nobody to go through and scored under the posts. Everybody said what a tremendous decision of mine to let play continue, but I look back on that now with absolute horror! Because the illegalities that must have gone on to get the ball out of that pile-up must have been nobody's business, and two wrongs in a game of rugby never make a right! In such a situation there is no semblance of advantage law whatsoever, because in a pile-up, 99% of the time someone is breaking the law to get the ball. There is only one way really that a player can play Laws 18 and 19 correctly, and that is to stay on his feet. Too often you see a player fall on his back and lie there, waiting and wondering when the support's coming, instead of doing something with the ball, which Law 19 requires them to do.

The tackle occurs when a player carrying the ball is held by an opponent and he is taken down to the ground, or the ball touches the ground. Now the only thing that the tackled player can do, the law says straight, is to release the ball and not only that, he must get away from it. If he releases, but then curls up and protects the ball, then it's a penalty straightaway. He must get away. Nor can he discriminate who he releases it to. Now, if the tackled player makes the effort to get away and the tackler stops him, it's a penalty against the tackler; he has got the first responsibility to get away. Once he is down there and the ball has touched the ground, he cannot play that ball at all; both tackled and tackler must get up onto their feet before they can play it.

Now that is clear-cut, yet we still have problems with it, simply because the referee is too slow getting there. Get there quickly, and make a decision as quickly as possible. Think of what they are doing:

(a)   Has he released the ball?
(b)   Is he getting away from it?
(c)   Has he been released to get away from it?

If a player is held on the ground, it is a tackle even though the ball has not touched the ground. He can't pull it in, and the tackler must not stop him from releasing the ball. Then the important thing is to look at the next player on the scene. If he dives straight on the top of the players on the ground, that is killing the ball and automatically a penalty against him. What this player should do is to stand over the top and either form a platform for his support players to drive over, or he should attempt to pick the ball up; if he is prevented from picking it up, then you must penalise the player on the ground who is stopping him from picking it up.

In the case of a smother tackle, when they both go to the

ground and the ball is held, the man that I look to penalise straightaway if he doesn't do anything is the tackler, because his objective is to kill the ball. It is going to be rather harsh if you apply that all the time, and I would also look to see what the tackled player is doing, but this is the situation that causes the most problems, because by the time we have thought who was responsible, other players have come in, they have all dived on top and we have one almighty mess on the floor. Some referees believe that in this situation following a smother tackle, a scrummage is a fairer way to start play rather than dishing out a penalty and a possible three points, but if we are going to listen to the pleas from the players, the boos from the crowd when we give the penalty, then yes, the pile-up will always be with us. Players should know that they are infringing the law when they are trying to kill the ball. If we are prepared to be ruthless, to be a referee and arbiter and make a decision and not just get out of it, then we will get rid of the pile-up worldwide. You might be right 90% of the time and wrong 10% of the time, but you will find that players are reluctant to go to ground in case they are that 10%, and they will stay on their feet and we'll get more fluent rugby. That is what I want as a coach, that is what I want as a referee, that is what I want as an occasional player (no it's not – I want the game slowed down when I play!), that is what the players want, unless they have lied when they have asked us when we are going to take action to get the pile-up out of the game. Remember, you can only play rugby on your feet; you can't play when you are on your back.

Let us look now at the first support player to arrive at the tackle. What is that player doing? Is he trying to play the ball, or is he trying to kill the situation? This is the individual referee's decision on the day, but if you feel that he is there to kill the ball, you penalise him. Similarly, if he comes in, goes to ground and holds the ball up just a little bit for the next man coming in, although he may be trying to get at the ball and get the game to flow, he is infringing Law 19 – lying on or near the ball – which says he has got to get up onto his feet. Support players coming in on their knees and wrestling for the ball have been a major cause of pile-up problems. In a nutshell, a player must not wilfully fall on or over another player who is lying on the ground near the ball, or on other players lying on the ground with the ball between them.

To go back to basics, though, if we react properly to the first two players there, the third player will not be a problem, because if the tackled player has released the ball and the tackler has allowed him to do so, there is no way that the third player is going to dive in when he can stand up for it.

We can now move on to the ruck and the maul. First the ruck. A player has gone to ground, he has released the ball according to the law but, due to the speed of the game, the players have come into contact over the top of him. Now in this situation the only way for a player to play that ball is with his feet: he can't use his hands, he can't use his head, he can't collapse it, at all times he must stay on his feet. The off-side lines are clear-cut for the threequarters, that is the hindmost foot. Whether the ruck moves right around or not, the hindmost foot off-side line, as it is interpreted in Great Britain, is always parallel to the goal line. Now referees get too involved in this situation and tend to forget what's next, because if the ball is emerging from the ruck correctly, referees are so intent on looking there that they forget the old swivel-head. The first thing a referee looks for is the ball, but once he has got sight of it, he should ask himself, what are the players doing who are coming into the ruck situation? Are they coming from their own side? Are they binding with at least one arm around the body of a player? When you see that they are coming in correctly and you see the ball coming out, don't forget to use the swivel-head.

The normal position that is adopted at the ruck is alongside it on the open side. A better position would be on the blind side, keeping your eye on the ball and looking infield where you can see the threequarters lined up. A superb position is back about six or seven yards from the ruck on the side who look like winning it. Make sure that the full-back isn't standing behind you, because if the scrum-half passes back to him for a clearance kick, you're going to receive the ball. But you can see the players on the fringe of the ruck, you can see the off-side line, and when the ball comes out, it should be only a matter of a quick spurt and you are up with play.

The position to adopt at the maul is the same as at the ruck, always remembering the swivel-head. The maul is set up with one player carrying the ball, one player from the opposition and one player from his own team – that is a maul. When the perfect maul is set up, with the ball-carrier protected by at least one blocker legitimately bound in on either side of him, there is no way that an opponent can get that ball. If he gets it somehow, he cannot have done so legitimately and therefore he must be off-side. But if one player has the ball and two opponents come in, that is not a maul, it is open play. Similarly, it is not a maul if no member of the opposition is in contact with the ball-carrier. This is very important because it now means that players can come in from any angle to receive the ball without being off-side. I did see a kick-off where a player called for the ball, caught it and the block went in immediately. Now, the opponents did not create a maul because they didn't make contact, so that all we had was one player holding the ball and two players of his own side quite legitimately binding. A forward from the kicking-off side ran round, pinched the ball, went down the field and scored the try. His opponents were absolutely amazed and, being English, were saying, 'Come on, there's a good chap. Give us the ball back, you're off-side.' But they were wrong – it wasn't a maul and, quite correctly, the try was given.

14

Coaching the Backs

by PIERRE VILLEPREUX

One of the great French full-backs of modern times, Pierre Villepreux played 29 times for his country between 1967 and 1972. He turned to coaching upon retirement and was a professor of physical education for some years at Toulouse, then national coach in Italy.

The four major virtues a back must have are the abilities:

1 To see or scan
2 To understand the result of his seeing
3 To be able to decide on an action
4 To be able to act positively on his decision.

The successful performance of the last of these indicates skill. Skill can be enhanced by both unopposed and opposed practices, but tactical decision-making and the encouragement of intelligent thinking can be fully developed only by putting players under the pressure of opposition. By this means, it is important that a coach creates activities and situations that enable the player to 'see' the game and make the best decision. Thus, from scrummage or lineout you have the same basic situation, with seven players marking seven players, and it is necessary also to mark four against four, three against three and even one against one. But second-phase play creates other situations – for example, from broken play not all defenders are necessarily facing you – so decision-making becomes vital, and practices simulating such situations must be included in a coaching session with backs. Give the players the ball and let them choose their play. The players without the ball have to take up good positions and to judge whether flat or deep alignment off the ball will bring the better results; good alignment is vitally important.

Beyond this, the only definitive advice that can be given on coaching the backs is not to waste such individual flair as you may be fortunate enough to have at your disposal by confining it in a rigid system of pre-set ploys and moves. Encourage the players to think for themselves. Otherwise, the only limits to a coaching session are the limits of your own imagination and the talent available. What follows, then, is just one set of graded exercises which might usefully make up a typical coaching session.

Exercise 1
British backs tend to pass the ball early, with the weight on the opposite foot and the shoulders at an angle to the man being drawn (Fig. 22). While facilitating the dummy, it leads to the threequarter line drifting outwards, depriving the winger of space and allowing a defender to mark more than one attacker. The French, on the other hand, attempt to draw the defender very close before releasing the ball. Feet positions are similar to the British method but the ball is delivered later and the body weight is much more evenly distributed between left and right foot because of the running line. The receiver is also encouraged

Fig. 22

to angle in towards the passer so that a straight running line is maintained. He takes the ball early with outstretched hands and swings it away with shoulders parallel to the goal line. If the French method is performed competently then the defence can in no way drift across. Exercise 1 is to practice this method in groups of four.

Exercise 2

In groups of four, the backs run across the field between the goal line and the 22-metre line, passing as in exercise 1, but on turning at the end each group is faced with rows of fours coming in the opposite direction, and has to continue with its passing. The great virtue of this exercise is that the returning group of four players is faced with an oncoming group, thus encouraging 'seeing' and decision-making. At all times great emphasis must be put on passing the ball in front of the receiver, on keeping running lines straight and flat alignment. To keep the straight running line, the receiver moves in towards the passer. This exercise sharpens the players' reactions and develops early concentration at the outset of the session.

Exercise 3

The backs line up conventionally, but no. 10 does not move a muscle until no. 9 has passed, no. 13 does not move at all until no. 10 has the ball, and so on (Figs. 23 and 23a). There is no movement whatsoever by the receiver until his immediate passer has the ball. Keep shouting that the ball must be moved in a flat trajectory and that the players must work for a good position before they receive the ball. The aim of this exercise is to ensure that the ball is moved quickly from its source, and that early and unprofitable running from bad positions is discouraged. Keep flat and time your run!

Exercise 4

Another exercise in straight and timed running. Starting in a straight line, each player arcs around to receive the pass, turning the line through ninety degrees. It's hard work! Instead of continuing in an arc, each player must angle inwards when taking the ball – no outward drift. This means that the further away from the initial ball position the runner is, the harder he has to work to keep on a straight running line. I make no apologies for emphasising that the receiver must angle in to the passer; it is essential for swift movement of the ball.

Fig. 23

Fig. 23a

Fig. 24

Fig. 25

Exercise 5

Here a defender is brought into a situation. The defender passes the ball out and then moves across to each receiver (Fig. 24). Each passer must attempt to control and 'fix' the movement of the defender by the timing of his pass, holding the ball until the last possible moment. If the defender is able to move successfully from one passer to another with a good chance of stopping the accurate movement of the ball, then the attackers are not performing as well as they must.

Exercise 6

Here there are three defenders in close proximity to two sets of attackers, and two in deeper positions, as in Fig. 25. The defenders can tackle, and decisions have to be made by the attackers as to where to move the ball. The coach should require such speed of ball movement as to put additional pressure on the attackers. To say that defence is 50% of the game seems a truism but very often it is neglected in sessions. In this exercise and in exercise 7, press the defenders constantly to 'see' and to react to the situations that arise. Defenders must keep close to the attackers and cut down their time.

Exercise 7

As soon as a player is tackled, he has to release the ball and all his supporting backs must converge on the ball. The opposition then move the ball in whichever direction they wish and the original attackers now have to fan and defend. The two sides alternate in ball possession. All the previous points are emphasised constantly: speed, running lines, alignment, quick defence, decision-making and decisive actions.

Exercise 8

The attacking scrum-half runs laterally in either direction, and the coach shouts to one of the defenders to tackle him (Fig. 26). The attackers must then choose the attacking option which offers them the best chance of success, and the defenders must react (Fig. 26a). It is essential here that there is no 'popping up' of the ball – it must be released. Occasionally, withdraw the defenders ten metres so that a lineout situation is simulated. Are the new options used widely?

Exercise 9

This exercise (Figs. 27 and 27a–b) is designed to encourage the counterattack. The defenders who find themselves behind the

Fig. 26

Fig. 26a

Fig. 27

Fig. 27a

Fig. 27b

opposition when there is a breakdown of play have to work hard to get behind the ball and into an on-side position. They must be ready to turn what seems to be an unprofitable position into one of attacking potential.

In all these exercises, bring on fresh defenders occasionally to maximise the pressure on attackers. If in the opposed activities the defenders are marking tightly, then encourage swift movement of the ball. If, however, the defenders have not been able to get into tight marking positions, then attackers must run to exploit this lack of defensive organisation. Again, it is the player who decides and exploits frailties in the opposition.

15

Observing and Assessing Referees

by JOE FRENCH

Joe French played first-grade rugby in Brisbane 1934–40 and represented Queensland 1935–36. After serving in World War II, he coached first-grade clubs 1946–53 and then Queensland 1949 –51. A Queensland selector 1954–59 and a national selector 1960–69, he has managed Wallabies touring teams on three occasions. In 1975 he was appointed to the Referees' Selection Panel, on which he still serves.

As a manager of several Australian national teams, I've had the privilege of observing some very great referees, such as Pat Murphy from New Zealand in 1964, Roger Vanderfeld from Australia in the late 1960s and early 1970s, Larry Lamb in France in 1971 and in 1972 John Pring. All of these gentlemen were top-class, always 'up-with-the-play' referees. None of them could ever have earned the nickname of 'Cinderella', as a referee did during my playing days for the very good reason that it was noticeable that he never quite got to the ball. Now it has been said many times that the game of rugby is not an exact science, and I suppose we should thank God for that, but it also follows that refereeing the game can't be labelled an exact science. Despite this, by hard labour and dedication the gentlemen I have named, and other top-class referees, have developed a natural, raw and basic instinct into a pleasurable skill or art.

From the moment he decides to give the game he loves the benefit of his assistance in the area he feels he is best suited for, to the moment he retires from active duty, the referee finds himself exposed to a degree of continual scrutiny, particularly in these days of TV, not experienced by the administrator or the player.

A player or administrator might contest that, but the referee accepts the fact that he is required to perfect his study of the laws, to submit himself to examination, advice, supervision, observation and assessment of his ability, to be physically fit, fleet of foot, polite, close-mouthed, impeccably dressed, courageous and ethically perfect. Canonisation is not far behind! In addition to this, he is required to endure the vocal criticism of those spectators who firmly believe that rugby is a game requiring thirty players, two touch judges and 5,000 referees! For eighty minutes, on behalf of all those connected with the code, he carries the full burden of being sole judge and jury and decision-maker.

To help this man in the area he has chosen to serve the cause of rugby, observation and assessment may be used to fulfil both his personal desire for efficiency and enjoyment, and his most important function of contributing to the players' enjoyment. A judgement of his performance, and any advice proffered thereafter, will of course vary according to whether such judgement is being made for a recruit or inexperienced referee, for promotional purposes, or for appointment to a representative game.

For each purpose the referee must be viewed in a different way, must be assessed in a different way and must be advised in a different way. Many Boards and individual assessors fail to appreciate this difference, thus creating a fundamental problem in the appointment of referees.

It is generally agreed that it is not essential to have played the game before beginning a refereeing career, but the advantage of having played is obvious. Opinion is that few players who have represented at the highest level take up the whistle, in my country anyway. An exception to this comes to mind in ex-All Black Frank McMullen, who has been quoted as saying that he found refereeing more difficult than playing because as a referee he had no immediate team-mates to support and comfort him in adversity. Now, being alone and unsupported, the referee is confronted with more challenges than the player and the first occurs before he even steps onto the field with the whistle. This is the challenge of learning the laws of the game thoroughly in theory. Then there is the prospect of having to apply the laws during a game, and this is the troublesome time: when the whistle is required to convert theoretical knowledge into a practical decision. The novice referee can be forgiven during his period of baptism for demonstrating his knowledge of the laws by frequent use of the whistle. It might be advisable for the assessor at this stage to remind him that he should also bring into play not only his knowledge of the laws, but also his knowledge of the object of the game as set out in his law-book.

A thorough knowledge of the laws is not the only element in an assessment of a referee's potential, although it is the ideal foundation. A correct attitude to the game is also essential – after the laws have been mastered there should come a genuine desire to influence and encourage the players to meet their objectives. Players react favourably when they sense that into their midst is come one who is not against any one of them, but who is working with them in trying to lift a game from the ordinary to a high standard of achievement and enjoyment. It is necessary, therefore, to involve all referees as often as possible in coaching seminars so that they may become aware of and increase their practical knowledge of the technical developments of the game.

It is important that the laws be applied equally to both teams. Human nature being what it is, there is an occasional tendency for the inexperienced to apply the full force of the law to one team only, not because of bias but unconsciously for some other reason such as a natural tendency to favour the underdog. To observe a referee applying the laws equally and fairly and at the same time displaying a feeling for the game is to see one referee who will soon whistle himself to the top. Add to this the necessary ingredients of neat appearance, fitness, speed, good positional play and sensible use of the advantage law, and the stage is set for the game to flow and the object of the game to be achieved.

There is very little need to emphasise that neat dress and clean appearance are important to a referee's image. Clean and freshly-ironed gear denotes self-respect and respect for the game. There is, however, a pressing need to insist upon a high degree of physical fitness since nothing irritates players more than to see a referee arriving late at a critical period of play and making guesswork decisions that may deny territory or even scoring opportunities. No unfit referee can expect to operate efficiently; by being up with the game he engenders player confidence and lessens any tendency for trouble to break out. All referees must be prepared to train regularly and continuously, since the reflexes, sound positional play, consistency, control and confidence are all enhanced by top fitness.

Sound positional play forms the basis for the skills and perception of a referee. Commonsense positioning comes with experience, and although the standard positional procedures can be read about in all the books designed to assist the newcomer in the early stages of his refereeing career, at the same time they leave him with the option of working out eventually and progressively what he may consider suitable to his style of refereeing. The important thing is that he must be in the right place at the right time and that he must arrive quickly without any undue interference with the movement of play. The only specific point I would make is to support what Alan Hosie has written at the end of chapter 6: near the goal line, the referee must position himself in the in-goal area so that play approaches him, thus avoiding the possibility of being unsighted at the vital moment of the ball being grounded by either side.

The newcomer referee will always be anxious to discover what judgements have been made of his performance. The primary objective of the assessor is to convey to him a feeling that he is being encouraged to improve his skills, so emphasis must first be placed on the favourable aspects of his game, followed by constructive criticism of the areas in which he might be remiss. The assessor should have a few beers with him afterwards, telling him nicely the areas in which he has been excellent and those where improvement is needed. His own development and promotion will depend entirely upon his own attitude and dedication but a sympathetic and sensitive approach to his problems by the assessor should motivate him to continue with his best endeavours.

Turning now to the assessment for promotion, I will first describe briefly the system used in Australia for the grading and promotion of referees. Each state or territory has its own referee organisation which is affiliated to the parent body. These referee organisations are also affiliated to the Australian Society of Rugby Referees which in turn is affiliated to the Australian Rugby Football Union, having representation thereon but without a vote. Each referee association is responsible for the grading and appointment of its active members to club games. In the State of Queensland the Queensland Referees' Association classifies referees into divisions 1, 2 and 3 plus a further unclassified group. Games are classified under the same headings and appointments made by an Appointments Board of three in accordance with gradings. The Queensland Classification Committee views referees in action as often as possible, written reports are furnished and the referee informed of the contents. No special report form is used: the referee is judged in the context of his grading and his strengths and weaknesses highlighted. Amendments are made to the classification list twice a year at a meeting of the combined Classification Committee and Appointments Board. By means of fortnightly discussions and lectures, the aim of the Queensland Classification Committee is to improve the standard of refereeing in all divisions.

By contrast, Sydney Rugby Referees' Association comprises a head body with fourteen affiliated referees' associations. The head body appoints to 185 games of senior, club and schools football each weekend. The affiliated bodies appoint to an even larger number of games, ranging from under-18 to under-6, sub-district and other minor football. The Sydney Referees' Association employs an Appointment Board comprising a maximum of nine ex-referee members, one of whom is a representative of the Sydney Rugby Union. The Board is divided into a major board comprising three members including the representative of the Sydney RU, and a minor board comprising a balance of the members. The major board appoints to the top four grades of senior club football, whilst the minor board is responsible for appointments to other games. The boards sit together to hear reports on referees who have been assessed the previous weekend, and then separate into two groups to appoint for the following weekend. Members of the board are expected to view four referees each Saturday. There is also a supplementary sighting panel consisting of senior active referees and other ex-senior referees. After a game the Appointments Board or sighting panel member will discuss performance with the referee and furnish a written report to the Board, a copy of which is sent to the referee. This is on a form which produces a longer and more complex report than the Queensland system. It establishes whether the referee is above the standard at which he is graded (Sydney referees are graded into eight divisions), equal to his current grading or below his current grading. An above-standard report will result in a special sighting for promotion, and a below-standard report will result in a special viewing for demotion.

Throughout Australia, all the normal criteria for acceptable refereeing, as previously dealt with, together with personality, bearing, coolness under pressure and attitude to the game are given full weight in making recommendations for promotion. Experience has shown that to promote too early generally results in permanent loss of confidence which can have a shattering effect upon the ambitious referee. However, where definite potential and aptitude are spotted by an assessor confident in his judgement, the aspiring referee should be given higher opportunity as soon as possible. In a way, a decision is being made on each referee once a week because the boards and associations have to do two things: review the assessments that have been made and appoint referees for coming games. In general they just leave things as they are, but about halfway through the year they have a good look and might up or down a few.

A referee should be assessed only on his form in the current season: like a footballer, if his form falls off in one year then he should be demoted in that year. You have got to look at him from the time the season starts, and if he has improved, fine; if he hasn't, he stays where he is.

The assessors themselves must be referees who are totally acceptable to the referees who they are assessing. They must have reached such a stage of refereeing that they have experienced the problems that are being faced by those referees they are judging. This is a pre-requisite before any assessor is appointed to the panel. Having got onto that panel, in the early part of his assessing career he must be taken through the various guidelines which have been mapped out over the years that the assessment panel has been in operation.

Assessors have their own strengths and weaknesses, and just in the same way as they were individualistic in their refereeing, so very often they will be individualistic in their assessment. Nevertheless consistency is highly desirable and assessors in a small country such as Wales are fortunate in that they can all get together at a game several times during the course of the season, do a common assessment and then discuss their problems and try to arrive at a uniform approach. It is not so easy to obtain uniformity of assessment between California and New York, British Columbia and Toronto, or even Brisbane and Sydney.

In chapter 21, Sam Williams will deal in some detail with the card system of assessing referees, whereby the clubs fill in report cards and they are sent back to a computer which assesses the result and grades accordingly. Since both teams fill in a card, any influence that the result of the game might have on the winners' or losers' assessment of the referee is cancelled out. The system also shifts onto the clubs some of the responsibility for helping to improve refereeing standards, and they have to be educated in what to look at before they give their marks. The most important thing as far as the clubs are concerned is to find one man to do the job and keep to him; then you get a fair consistency. In my view, there is no need for such a system if there are enough assessors to go around; if there are not, then the cards are a useful background that puts referees in approximate order. But throughout the season the assessors should have been looking as well, and it must be the assessors' opinion which counts at the end of the season.

Finally, let me return to my own country and how referees are selected for representative games in Australia. The three-man Australian Referees' Selection Committee comprises one nomination from the Australian Rugby Football Union with two others being elected at the Annual Meeting at the beginning of the year from nominations received from affiliated bodies. The Australian Referees' Selection Committee does not necessarily include a member of the Australian Society of Referees, but as a matter of arrangement and as a matter of understanding between the delegates, the nomination of the Australian Society of Referees is always elected to the Selection Committee. At the start of a season of semi-international and Test matches, the Selection Committee selects a national panel of referees comprising eight or ten current or potential Test referees. From these the Selection Committee appoints referees to all semi-international games, international school games and the annual Inter-state Queensland v. New South Wales game. For Test matches it has been customary in recent years for a panel of three referees to be submitted to the touring management for consideration. By arrangement, the touring team will have played under each of the panel prior to the first Test. This system can vary, not least with the welcome growth in the use of neutral referees.

At this level the Selection Committee looks for first-class anticipation and positioning, ability to read the game, coolness under pressure, ability to invoke the advantage law and courage in dealing with foul play. The hallmark of top refereeing under all playing conditions is the ability to apply the advantage law sensibly, strengthened by alert positioning and the ability to read the game. The indefinable ability to read the game comes from experience and as a process of a constant study of team character-istics and tactical moves combined with a deliberately acquired knowledge of the personal habits and abilities of individual players. Coolness under pressure will determine the degree of control and add to the ability to meet the difficulties that will inevitably and suddenly occur in top-class rugby.

Our game of rugby has broadened its base and developed and advanced its cause throughout the world by a proper blending of the endeavours of the three arms of its basic structure: the administrator, the player and the referee. All three share equally

143

in the right to enjoy the game, but this right is accompanied by responsibilities each to the other and the role of the referee is becoming increasingly important to the image of the game displayed to the world. Application of the laws without the exercise of restraint kills the game as a spectacle and destroys the sport as a means of enjoyment. The real skills and the art of refereeing lie in achieving a balance between firmness, impartiality, fairness and commonsense. So long as these qualities are looked for and encouraged in a referee, the influence of our referees upon the advancement of the game will improve and lead to greater enjoyment of the game by all concerned.

16

Mini-Rugby

by J. MALCOLM LEWIS

Holder of a St Luke's College Diploma in Physical Education, Malcolm Lewis played for Bristol and Coventry, coached Coventry and has been Assistant Coaching Organiser for the Welsh Rugby Union since 1973.

Teachers and coaches of very young players have an awesome responsibility. They must ensure that those young players derive enjoyment from the game through success (which is not necessarily the same thing as winning); they must encourage individual flair and not just pay lip-service to it; they must teach technique in the basics of handling, running, contact and kicking, and develop it into skill by judiciously applied pressure; they must organise practice sessions which are fun and in which everyone is involved; they must get across the fundamental team principles of going forward, support, continuity and pressure. How well teachers and coaches achieve these objectives will determine whether their young charges stay in the game at all, and if so, what success they enjoy in it.

To help coaches of comparatively new players, there is a game which those players can enjoy once they can handle and run under a certain amount of pressure. It is called mini-rugby and is a simple game in which youngsters have a chance to show their skills without too much pressure. A lot of time was spent in devising this form of the game and in making it simple enough for the youngsters to understand, even for the teacher to understand. The full rules are to be found in an RFU publication called *Mini-Rugby*. The one thing not to forget is that the game is only an introduction and that we are dealing with beginners. Do not throw them right into the deep end far too early.

145

Mini-rugby is a game for nine players. It is very important in playing or coaching this game to understand why the positions for those nine players were thought out; if they are not understood, then the game will suffer. At the same time, never try to label a child a hooker, or a prop, or a scrum-half, because you don't know if in time he will make a hooker or a prop or whatever. Move him about for his own benefit; that's part and parcel of developing his game. At one session I took, the hooker said to me after I had asked them to inter-change positions, 'I've never played anywhere else, I don't even know where that is!' Now I think that's dreadful. Mix them up and play them all over the place, always remembering that it's a physical game so you should not put a little one against a big one in the scrum.

A hooker is played for obvious reasons because it is a specialist position. One prop is needed because when a scrum-half puts the ball into the scrum there must be a player on his side. A no. 8, or a lock, is the player behind them to hold them together. A flanker is there because the flanker in modern-day rugby is so important and his function is developing. The scrum-half and fly-half are included for obvious reasons because they are pivotal in the game. The other positions are centre, wing and full-back.

The four forwards make a unique set-up. There are a number of people who will disagree with two in the front row and will want three. But if another prop is included to make it three in the front row, then you have to put another lock in to hold him and you're missing out the whole of a back row, which is very important to the development of rugby football, and how are we going to teach back-row skills? If you like, stick a no. 8 in, which gives us six forwards, but we are still leaving out a flanker, as well as cluttering up the area, probably having more players than we want and exerting undue pressure on the youngsters. There is no satisfactory answer to putting in a tight-head prop: although he is very important in the fifteen-a-side game, do not forget that you are dealing with young beginners and all you are concerned with at the moment is a scrummage where they'll learn the techniques without having 8, 9, 10 or even 11-year-olds scrummaging for minutes on end. You want the ball in and out, trying to produce the skills that the youngsters are there for.

Fig. 28 shows the foot positions I like to see within the mini-rugby scrummage. Each player has a job to do and it is important that he learns it. The hooker has to learn where to put his feet. Children have most difficulty in understanding that they've got to move their right foot towards the ball to deflect it at

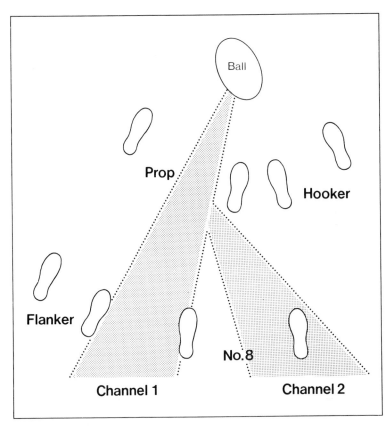

Fig. 28

first, not kick it back, nor heel it back with their heel, but to deflect it to be channelled through the legs of the prop. If the hooker tries to do that with his left foot he's got all sorts of problems. He has to reach for the ball and so his body position becomes awkward to push on and he cannot control his foot as well.

The loose-head also has problems with his feet more often than not. The natural thing for a learner to do is to put one foot in front of the other but that's not producing what we want: a tunnel for the ball. So put his feet in the position shown in Fig. 28 – wide apart. The flanker and no. 8 are there to push hard, watch the ball and control it. Again, their feet are wide apart. Once they have

147

mastered these roles, they can progress to back-row moves. When it is the opposition's put-in, the flanker is moved over to the other side. This not only balances the scrum but he has now become the right-hand flanker and is learning a different role. His team are now defending, and the same options are open to them as to the defenders in an eight-man scrum.

Ball channels are important. The ball has to come out without those youngsters feeling undue pressure, so we produce a channel between the legs of the loose-head, in between the flanker and the no. 8. The ball can come out quickly, or it can be controlled by the flanker's right foot and by the lock's left foot. Through channel 2, exactly the same as in the senior game, the ball is directed to the right-hand side of the no. 8.

Youngsters must be given simple instructions to follow. There are three questions a forward must think of at each scrum. Where do I put my feet? Where do I grip or bind? Where do I put my head and shoulders? The last question becomes very important because if he's got a problem it's usually to his neck and back, and that means he's screwed up or not in the right mechanical position. That's bad: the youngster must be comfortable and happy, because if he's uncomfortable and unhappy then he's not going to want to play. It's as simple as that. He's got to understand where to put his feet, where to grip and where to put his head and shoulders until it becomes habit. Then you can start to talk about the different heights that he scrummages, the different levels and the different players that he'll come up against and all sorts of things, but those three basics are as important to him as they are to any International. They are valuable lessons: feet, grip, and head and shoulders.

Most of this chapter has been spent on scrummaging, but it's such a unique part of the game and causes players and coaches such problems. Also, its importance in mini-rugby is increased by the absence of lineouts, although I feel that perhaps lineouts will be included before very long. I am a passionate believer in good lineout play, and the earlier the youngster understands this facet of play the better the lineout will be. Understanding the lineout laws is so important. Youngsters learn the lineout game far quicker and far easier through the shortened line, which of course is what they would have in mini-rugby.

Like the forwards, the backs have got to start learning their different functions. What is the role of the scrum-half? When you put him in that position, what do you expect from him? What do you expect from the fly-half? How far away does he stand? Why does he stand there? How important is it? How does he run? Similarly with the centre and wing and the roles of attack and defence, the roles of support with and without the ball. What is the full-back's role? How does he come up, why does he come up, when does he come up?

Mention of the scrum-half brings up another controversial question about how the game is played: the scrum-half on the side losing the ball at the scrummage may not follow the ball and harass his opposite number. There are those who feel that this removes from the forwards their responsibility for channelling the ball and that it gives scrum-halves a false sense of security, allowing them to develop bad habits. Maybe, but right at the beginning I would prefer the pressure to be kept off the scrum-half, even though the skill of passing should still be learned and improved.

There are variations in the rules concerning goal-kicking. The youngsters are usually allowed to kick in front of the posts, while the older ones kick as in the senior game, opposite wherever the try is scored. A drop-kick or place-kick can be used; some coaches allow only a drop-kick, but the place-kick plays such a part in our game that it is probably better to keep the choice.

Two final but fundamental points. First, the time: for eights or nines, a quarter of an hour each way is long enough, with an extra five minutes each way for eleven-year-olds. Second, the ball: playing with the right size of ball is very important. Youngsters find it very easy to catch a bigger ball and like playing with the bigger ball, but they cannot manipulate it in the way that they should. They will catch a bigger ball with all the bad habits, letting it come into the cradle and using their arms rather than their hands and fingers.

17

Problem Areas for Referees

by DENZIL LLOYD

Denzil Lloyd has given a long period of service to the game as a referee who achieved International honours and as an adviser off the field in recent years. He became a referee in 1958 and after several exchange matches was honoured with his first International at the age of 46. He has conducted clinics in the four Home Unions, France and Canada and is well-known in Europe for his rugby enthusiasm.

My years as a Welsh Rugby Union observer and assessor have shown me that referees (including some of the very top-rated ones) are having some consistent problems, so this chapter moves through the laws of the game and picks out a number of these basic difficulties.

The size of the field
This may not appear to be a particular problem. However, early in Bridgend's tour to Vancouver in 1972 they played a match on a field, the width of which was naturally restricted. It was fairly obvious that the wings were confined by the narrow field. In a later game the home coach deliberately asked for the pitch to be kept down to sixty yards. It was spotted, and as the teams took the field to the strains of National Anthems, the groundsman was extending the pitch by five yards! So take care to check the markings, particularly when soccer is also played on a ground. Some of the weird goal posts seen on the North American continent take a lot of getting used to as well; the advice is to play on if it comes back off the woodwork.

The ball
Here again there doesn't appear to be much of a problem, but in a Cardiff v. Llanelli match I refereed, at the first penalty kick a Llanelli player complained about the ball being flat. It was, and was kicked off, the next one was brought on and then another. Barry John tried to drop-kick them out but they were flat also. So we were in the embarrassing position of having to wait in a senior game whilst the balls were pumped up again. I just didn't check.

Number of players
Do we ever check the number? Many years ago I was asked to referee a District Union Cup match. The visiting team turned up three short about half an hour late for a Wednesday evening game. The home team (Pontrhydyfen, famous for being the birth-place of Richard Burton), agreed to loan them three men. We proceeded to walk the threequarters of a mile from the clubhouse to the ground and began the match. At the first lineout the visiting captain said, 'We have nine forwards' (wings used to throw the ball in in those days), so I said, 'One will have to leave.' He called, 'Winger, go off.' At the next line we only had seven players in the lineout – two of the borrowed players were on the wing and both had gone off the field. The captain had one back on to play, but ten minutes later, when running past me, he said, 'This one's no good. Can I have the other one back!' So count the players.

Special regulations
It is as well to point out here that you should know your own District's rules relating to competitions and if you move to other areas you should certainly check. I remember refereeing at the Selkirk Sevens in the Border District of Scotland. I had completed one game allowing a minute interval and then heard one of the Scottish referees telling the captains at the toss, 'Don't forget there is no interval.' Once again, I just hadn't checked. On another occasion I was at Stradey Park for a Floodlight Alliance final, Llanelli v. Ebbw Vale. It was a beastly night and before the toss Carwyn James came and asked me what would happen if the game was abandoned. I didn't know the rules but assured him it would not be abandoned. However, in the 61st minute I had to call a halt as several of the players were suffering from exposure. Nobody on the ground knew the rules but eventually it was found that the score stood after 60 minutes. However, Ebbw Vale agreed to a replay of the first leg of the two-legged final, lost

151

heavily and couldn't win by enough points in the return game to win the final.

Half-time
A practice certainly not seen in Britain is taking place in South Africa, where at half-time they come off the field to a table close at hand and take orange juice. The referees say the playing enclosure is the field of play plus a reasonable area surrounding. The practice is to be frowned upon because the players who leave the field can take instructions from their coaches.

Incidentally, when the Welsh Soccer XI played the Welsh Rugby XI (or was it XIII?), Gareth Edwards suggested that when the soccer players went off at half-time as was their custom, the rugby players should have stayed on and scored as many goals as they could during the interval!

Players' dress
The old days of the harness seem to have gone, thank goodness, and the International Board's ruling on maximum and minimum dimensions seems to have gone some way to solving the problem of studs. Nevertheless, studs should still be inspected, as should the plastic edge on the front of some boots, worn down to a razor's edge. Sharp, damaged eyelets on boots are also worth looking at.

When to toss up
Some countries will toss up twenty minutes before the start of the game, whilst others will toss in the tunnel to the field or even on the field itself. The significant point is not when the toss up is conducted, but when should the winning captain be obliged to reveal his decision. Some referees believe that the winning captain should tell the other captain of his intentions immediately the result of the toss-up is known; others feel that a decision should be made on the field itself, since to be made to reveal one's intentions immediately after the toss-up leads to an unfair situation.

Referee and touch judges
I must confess that when it was first mooted that touch judges should help referees in enforcing Law 26 (3), I was very much against it, believing in Law 6 (5), that wonderful phrase, 'The Referee is the Sole Judge of Fact and Law'. Following certain happenings in the game, however, I had to concede that one pair

152

of eyes were insufficient to control certain types of games. The fear of a handful of top referees, that we would have flag-waving maniacs, proved an insult to the excellent exchange referees who act as touch judges.

It is important to remember that touch judges only flag in cases of Law 26 (3) and there must be a caution or sending off. The only exception to this is when a touch judge can identify an offending team but not an individual, and even then I suppose the referee should issue a general warning to the captain or the pack, depending on the incident.

It also needs to be emphasised that there is no intention of the touch judges making any further decisions other than on Law 26 (3).

Advantage

Although the debate about advantage continues, the use of it seems to separate the great from the ordinary referee. In Wales we have never liked the long advantage played by visiting referees (principally the SRU referees) but certainly the best use of advantage we have seen at the National Stadium in recent years has been in the performances of Mr Alan Hosie. His use of advantage was absolutely consistent. The players knew exactly where they were and, wonder of wonders, the spectators knew as well. Perhaps, then, this is the vital key in the playing of advantage – consistency.

A thought here: why is Law 24 A(1) Note relating to off-side so explicit? If the advantage is not gained the penalty should in all cases be awarded even if it is necessary to bring play back for that purpose to the place of infringement. Why is it stressed so much in this law?

Kick-off

There is no particular problem here, except that senior referees should be cautious in telling new referees about unorthodox positions at the kick-off. With their experience they can afford to adopt these positions, and as long as they work, good luck to them.

It is quite disappointing in this phase to see lots of referees not playing advantage at the kick-off, and when this happens in Sevens it is sacrilege to me.

Here brief mention could be made of the non-maul already touched on by Clive Norling in chapter 13. One player of the non-kicking-off side runs behind the players receiving, his own players do not close up (deliberately) and he can wreak havoc on the 'wrong' side of his opponents. Too often this is penalised for off-side as if he had formed the maul.

Penalty try

There has been quite a debate about one particular aspect. A player fields the ball in-goal and knocks it on to one of his own team standing in front of him. He catches it, thereby preventing the opponents scoring a try. For some reason people will not accept this as foul play, wilfully offending against a law of the game. It must be a penalty try.

A harder situation to judge is when the defending team knocks on when going for an interception near their own line during a handling movement by the attackers. If a penalty try is awarded, it can seem that the punishment exceeds the crime. A way in which this can be interpreted and a decision taken is that if the player going for the interception has his palms upwards and is using both hands, he would seem to have the intention of catching the ball. If his palms are down and he is using only one hand, there is no way that he will catch it.

Off-side

This law is played well in open play, but there is one aspect that is either ignored or played badly: the ten-metre law is hardly ever operated when the scrum-half chips over the top of the lineout and the pack keep charging ahead.

What of the player who is off-side, within ten metres but nearer his opponents' goal line? If he retired he would embarrass the receiver, so should we not expect him to get outside the ten-metre circle by the shortest possible route? It is well to remember, however, that if there is no player waiting to play the ball but one arrives, then the opponents within ten metres are not obliged to retire but must not obstruct or interfere with him.

Finally, what of a planned strategy of a high kick by the full-back and everyone in an off-side position runs to the ten-metre line, forming a sort of wall across the field? By law there is nothing at all wrong with this but if one can use the phrase, does it seem correct morally?

Scrummage

The first priority is to establish the team responsible for the stoppage of play. If a player has an opportunity or a moment when he can release the ball, but chooses to hold it and drive into a maul situation, then he is responsible for the stoppage and consequently loses the right of put-in at the scrummage. If this law was operated properly, it would produce freer rugby, with the ball being moved more frequently.

Next, the question of the wheeling scrum and a player leaving the scrum in front of the off-side line. There is a clear ruling that when the scrum has turned through 180°, only the last man is allowed to detach, pick up and play on. What of the scrum that turns through anything less than 180°: can the flanker pick it up in front of him or can he unbind and play it behind him? Is it permissible for a flanker to break under these circumstances provided he immediately retires to his original off-side line? Should there be a common philosophy about this without contracting out of law?

From a wheeling scrummage to a twisting scrum. This seems to be becoming a blight on the game. Some people say it is a constructive ploy, but I would prefer to see a method of outlawing it from the game. It is a difficult situation in which to apportion blame, but the mayhem resulting from twisting scrummages seems to engender a lot of 'aggro'.

In passing, it seems odd that whilst a scrum-half is prohibited from kicking through a scrum, a flanker correctly bound is quite entitled to do this provided he doesn't play the ball in the tunnel.

Scrum collapsing

This subject has been admirably dealt with by Alan Welsby in chapter 8, but I would just quote the Australian team that toured the UK in 1975. They were weak scrummagers and got away with collapsing in most of their games, but at Neath they were hammered by a strong referee in the first half and did not concede any penalties in the second half – there must be a moral here. The problem of deciding who is responsible is a very difficult one, but why should anyone want to collapse a scrum when they have the drive on and are moving forward?

Are players sophisticated enough to drop the scrum just to win penalties? Any doubts on this score were dispelled when I heard a coach recount a story of how a Welsh prop had done this for Gwent in 1970 when they beat the Springboks. It was part of a pre-match tactical plan.

What we do not want to see is scrum after scrum collapsing because the referee is busy scanning for off-side and not one scrum is penalised throughout the game. I have seen referees having really good games and completely ignoring this facet of play. Have a good look at body positions, binding and leg positions. On a wet muddy day it is feasible that scrums will go down with no wilful intent, but you should not play on from any collapsed scrum – either penalise or scrum again. Conversely, too many referees order re-scrums for other reasons when they should play on or penalise.

Now that touch judges can help in identifying foul play, it is interesting to note that one country is already suggesting that the touch judges should not switch sides at half-time so they observe different props in each half of the game.

Ruck and maul

Referees get much too close to these situations for good all-round vision. It is quite correct to search for the ball but not at the expense of everything else around these phases of the game. There is sometimes a frightening committal to the ruck after the ball has been located, and the use of the swivel-head is highly recommended.

Theoretically it is often difficult to determine a line through the hindmost foot as the ruck or maul is twisting, turning or breaking up. Do we really referee it in relation to joining in front of the ball, unbinding or rejoining behind the ball, or do we sensibly referee it in trying to establish the intent of the player? What about players joining it from the side, and how do we decide how legal players are when they drive straight through the ruck and maul, scattering players like ninepins? Referees accept that players must bind with one arm but nobody insists that it must be around players of their own side. Why is it there in law if people don't operate it?

Do referees accept that players must be bound in a maul also? Section 1 of this law states: A player is not in physical contact unless he is caught in or bound to the maul and not merely alongside it. Does the referee really have sufficient time or the desire to see that players are bound at ruck or maul?

Finally, one point about a conventional maul – in the setting up with the wedge made, a show-off joins in an exposed position. There is nothing wrong with an opposition player joining behind the ball and binding with the one arm whilst attempting to get the ball away from the opponent with the other.

Lineout

The lineout is said to end when play (except maul or ruck on the line of touch) moves outside fifteen metres or the last-man position. We never seem to consider it finished if it moves into the five-metre area.

A major criticism is the allowing of the last man of the non-throwing-in side stepping behind his opposite number and shading across the lineout at the same time. The ball lands in the lineout and he should be penalised. It is very difficult to spot from the front of the lineout but should be obvious at the back. This is not such a technical offence as some referees seem to think, because in stepping behind, the flanker has an open road to create havoc amongst the half-backs.

Is the half-metre gap roughly the correct distance or does it produce lateral jumping? It should be clear to all that a person is allowed to jump across the line of touch provided he is in the act of jumping for the ball, but not when he is about four men away from the jumper.

The quick throw-in doesn't appear to be much of a problem, as long as no-one but players handles the ball, but the scrummage law says that there should be three men from each side to form the scrum: should not the lineout law be as explicit and outlaw the quick throw-in from touch?

Movement by the last player up and down the line, coupled with players changing positions on the line of touch, is presenting some major headaches. What can we do to stop them or do we want to do anything to stop them? Is it correct to penalise the last player of the opponents for not moving up with him, or should it be a free kick for not throwing the ball in without delay? Does 'without delay' simply mean not feinting, or can we take the matter still further and penalise for wilful waste of time? The French penalised players changing position for leaving the line of touch until the International Board announced that this was not to be done. However, I personally believe that anything which delays the game should be penalised as there are too many things holding up the game already.

Is it worth having the peeling-off law in the book? It appears that nobody is operating it, and how can more than one man peel legally? Generally they are purely to drive and wedge.

Are parallel straight lines being maintained? A common feature now is the player stepping out of the line to have additional lateral momentum in jumping for the ball. The metre gap is not maintained and compression occurs. It is interesting to see the attention the French 'arbitres' pay to the metre gap; they frequently station themselves near the scrum-half position and indicate the gap they require before the ball is thrown in.

Some of the lineout problems I have discussed may seem only technical points in comparison to the punching, barging and general mayhem that takes place in the lineout. But not enough work is done in ensuring that the lines are parallel, the gaps are kept and so on, while observers frequently criticise referees for being static at the lineout. The problems of the lineout are still immense, as John Pring has shown in chapter 10, and the amount of criticism referees receive about the lineout may be due to more the law than to the referees. The good referee has a priority list of what to look for in the lineout, but even he should accept counselling if it is observed that he is continually missing any of the problems.

Penalty kicks
Referees do not position themselves well after awarding penalty kicks, and certainly it is an area where concentration is not 100%. Certain referees hurl their arms high in the air and swing around flamboyantly, while people are being trampled nearly to death only a couple of feet away from them. Some are distracted by opponents querying decisions and do not concentrate on the nature of the kick being taken; one can recall the famous free kick taken as a penalty at Murrayfield. Young referees concentrating on the forwards not being back ten metres miss the real villains of the piece – the backs who do not retire and float in for interceptions. In general not enough thought is given to moving quickly into a good position to have overall vision.

Sending off
I believe sending off is a gut reaction – 'You dirty so-and-so', and off he goes. If you've got to think about a sending-off, you don't send him, you take him to the side and talk to him. To talk to him and then send him off – I don't think that is good. It is usually very obvious what he's done, if it's the boot or the fist. Forget the old theory that sending a man off gets the referee into trouble; you should be so strongly supported that you will get into more trouble for not sending off a man who deserves to go.

18

Fitness for Players

by DON RUTHERFORD

The RFU's Technical Administrator since September 1969 and previously a schoolmaster, Don Rutherford was one of the outstanding England full-backs since the war. He made fourteen appearances for his country and toured with the 1966 Lions in New Zealand. His last International was against New Zealand in 1967. He has played an important part in organising coaching schemes throughout England and he's visited many countries, lecturing and studying the game.

Why play rugby? J. J. Stewart mentioned it in chapter 2: a love for the game. One of the supposed joys of rugby is that you don't necessarily have to be fit in order to play, in other words you can play coarse rugby and still get some enjoyment from it. However, there is a point at which even coarse rugby becomes dangerous, and you need a degree of fitness no matter what level you play.

There is an analogy between your body and a motor car, because there are parallels which must be understood: understand principles, then look at an individual and improve that particular individual. There are many different types of motor car, and many different types of body. Whilst there are guiding principles, you have got to look at each individual because each individual will be different. Pay particular attention to the fact that we are only as efficient as the food that we eat and our capacity to use oxygen.

To keep it simple, the body has two basic energy systems. The word 'aerobic' has confused an awful lot of people. Think of it as two words, 'with oxygen'. The aerobic capacity is the amount of oxygen the body can process within a given time. Everyone will be able to process oxygen at different rates and with different degrees of efficiency, but the larger the aerobic capacity, the greater the activity sustained. The ability to improve your aerobic system depends on being able to breathe rapidly large volumes of air, to deliver that oxygen to the bloodstream and for the bloodstream to deliver the oxygen to the muscles. The maximum oxygen uptake determines the level of aerobic output, and the level of work which a player is capable of sustaining. Working aerobically, therefore, can be defined as working at a steady state, or 'pay as you go'. Aerobic fitness is the basis of all fitness. The best way of improving it is by running; one view is that 16 minutes with a heart-rate of 120 is the optimum. This is something which the player can do on his own – the coach's time at a restricted training session is just too valuable.

Rugby is essentially an aerobic activity, but it also has strong elements of another energy system, the 'anaerobic system', i.e. 'without oxygen'. If the work load is much greater than the aerobic capacity, another energy source has to be called upon and this is what we call anaerobic. Work at the anaerobic level is very limited because the body runs into oxygen debt. You are soon aware of it; gasping for breath is an obvious sign that you are running into oxygen debt. During oxygen debt other biochemical changes within the body produce the necessary energy and these changes are reversible later in the presence of oxygen. So when you are feeling absolutely knackered you are breathing heavily, but gradually, as you are taking in more oxygen and processing it in your body, so your body returns to a steady state. When an athlete performs flat-out anaerobic work, sources are depleted in about forty seconds. Think, for instance, of a 100-metre sprint. Do you breathe as you are going along? The answer is no – in fact, it is probably 90% anaerobic, from a second source of energy that is being generated within your body.

The major difference between the analogy of the motor car and your body is that one of the wonderful properties of the body is its ability to improve with use. In other words, you don't lie on your back wishing to be a fitter rugby player, whereas a machine will, with use, actually wear down and become less efficient.

What is fitness for a rugby player? It is obviously different from the specific fitness required by a sprinter, or a shot-putter, or a 1500-metres runner, or a boxer, or a tennis-player. Elements of all these types of fitness are required, but the degree to which each player needs them will depend on the level of rugby he wishes to play, and in what position. To be more specific, although there is no precise definition of fitness for rugby, the eight components of fitness can be identified.

1 *Efficient heart and lungs*. Typically, a no. 8 forward would be expected to have good cardio-vascular (heart-lung) fitness for his functions of running, shoving, wrestling, jumping etc.
2 *Speed*. We instantly recognise those players who have got this quality, and it is a very important component of fitness.
3 *Dynamic strength*. For example, the lifting and turning of an opponent.
4 *Static strength*. Before the ball goes into the scrum, the two packs of forwards are apparently leaning on each other, but in fact they are resisting tremendous pressures by exercising their static strength.
5 *Explosive strength*. Chalk your fingers, jump up and see how far you can reach up a wall: the distance between your standing height and your jump height is a measure of explosive strength.
6 *Local muscular endurance*. The tremendous effort that is required to remove the ball when it is held in a maul or similar situation is local muscular endurance.
7 *Agility*. The side-step or swerve would be a good example of what we mean by agility.
8 *Flexibility*. For example, a pick-up from the ground where the player has to bend to execute a scrum-half type of pass. A pivot pass would be another example of flexibility.

The level to which each component is developed will vary according to the player and his position in the team. The coach must recognise the specific demands that the game makes on each position and structure the training programme to develop specific components of fitness. In Australia, wrestling coaches have been enlisted to help front-row forwards, and volleyball coaches to help lineout jumpers.

To assess the training programme's value in bringing about the improvement of the player's specific fitness, tests must be given to the players which will measure the level of each component at relevant times during the year. With such objective measures the coach can become more aware of his players' strengths and weaknesses, whilst at the same time assessing the benefits of his training programmes throughout the year. Also, the players can see fitness in terms of easily understood results: if you try and bamboozle them with too much science you are going to leave them stone dead. Link fitness training to the game so that they are never in any doubt as to why they are doing it.

Let us do just that now, and look at the demands of the game. This is, of course, where we all fall down rather rapidly because our knowledge is extremely slight. We do know that before the law-change affecting touch-kicking outside the 22, the ball was in play for 13–14 minutes, whereas it is now in play on average for 27 minutes. What is happening during the rest of the 80 minutes? We also know that 50% of the action on a rugby pitch lasts for less than 10 seconds, so a ball might be thrown into a lineout, there's a bit of sparring, the whistle goes, it's all over in 7 seconds. We start again. We scrum 15 metres in and there's another burst of action. On average there are forty scrums, of which 90% last up to 20 seconds, 50 to 60 lineouts, and 60 to 80 rucks and mauls.

If anyone feels like doing the rather laborious but very important analysis of the distances that players run and the speeds at which they run, they might help the development of the game considerably. In Australia they actually used a cine-camera to follow an inside centre throughout the game. They then analysed how far he had run and at what pace. He covered a total of 6,329 yards, including 54 sprints averaging 3.5 seconds each and covering 25–200 yards. This at least suggests good thinking behind one of the popular rugby training activities: sprinting from your goal line to your 22-metre line and back a number of times, to halfway and back a number of times to the far 22-metre line and to the far goal line and back. Similar work on prop forwards has highlighted the difference between levels: there is appreciably more sprinting required in an International than in a club match.

Just as there is a measure of agreement on the components of fitness, there is also a certain measure of agreement on the principles of training. The first one is the general principle that you need efficient heart and lungs. Then, you have got to be very *specific* and find out the training that is required for your sport, for rugby football. Next you have to look at the *individual positions*, as already discussed. One word of warning here: don't get too bogged down on too many specifics and have your wings doing so much speed work, or your front row so much work with weights, that they never develop their heart-lung fitness. For training to have any impact it must *overload* the system: if I am always lifting the same object, then I am certainly not going to be overloading my system. However, if I increase the weight, then obviously I am going to overload it gradually and I will see some improvement in my strength.

162

You have to impose demands on the body which are going to have relevance to what you are doing: jogging might be a marvellous activity in the summer for players just to keep in shape, but if they spend their time on jogging then all they are doing really is preparing themselves for an activity which is less severe than jogging; clearly that is useless because when you play rugby you know that the activity is more demanding than simply jogging. In order to achieve an improvement *progression* means that you never assume that the absolute peak of fitness has been or ever can be reached. It is linked with *reversibility*: once you stop an activity, your level of fitness just goes down, so it is a good idea to test a player who declares himself fit after a lay-off. If you've got his times for, say, a 600-metres run before an injury, give him the 600-metres run again and if he is five seconds slower you know for certain that he is not as fit as he was before the injury.

Measurement is very important from the point of view of motivation, as is *competition*. Finally, give your programme *variety*. A three-mile run is a three-mile run, but take it over different terrain: on the beach, through the woods, around the streets, around the pitch. You are still doing the same thing, but you are psychologically changing the activity for the players.

The most important thing of all to remember when coaching fitness is that it is a means rather than an end: you don't want a front-row with superb upper-body strength but no scrummaging technique, a volleyball player who is bundled out of every lineout, or a world-class sprinter who would be a useful winger if only he could catch the ball. On the other hand, as the fitness level drops, so does the skill level, so the fitness of his players is an aspect of coaching which no all-round coach will ignore.

19

Fitness for Referees

by LEIGHTON DAVIES

> *Leighton Davies played for Bridgend for twelve seasons and was captain in 1965/66, when the club championship was won. He also played for and captained Maesteg and later coached Bridgend. He is senior lecturer in PE at South Glamorgan Institute and a member of the WRU's Coaching Advisory Committee as well as a Staff Coach.*

The type of fitness with which referees have to be mainly concerned is cardio-vascular, that is fitness of the heart and lungs. Fitness is specific, so if you want to get really fit cardio-vascularly then you can swim, you can cycle, you can run; by such means you can become very fit cardio-vascularly, but it won't be muscle-specific. In order to be a runner you must run, to be a swimmer you've got to swim and so on. So the specific qualities of fitness for referees involve running in different degrees.

An analysis has been done of the amount of walking, jogging and running referees do in typical club matches in Wales (both junior and first-class games). We looked at the amount of time a referee spent running and how fast he ran, because there are different qualities necessary for a medium-pace kind of training programme and for a fast one. For the medium-pace running you need a quality called aerobic fitness. All this means is that you are able to work for a long period of time at a continuous pace such that the oxygen debt you incur whilst working is repaid. Now at other times, when you have to run much faster, you need what we call anaerobic efficiency; usually, if you sprint fifty yards, then you have to rest something in the order of about twenty or thirty seconds, depending on your state of fitness, to recover.

When the results of our analysis were collated, we found that the average distance covered were: walking 800 yards; jogging or medium-pace 2,640 yards; and fast pace about 1,320 yards.

We now know what the work load is likely to be on the poor referee, and we can look at some training programmes that would be suitable for him in order to referee the particular type of game we analysed (it is obviously likely that the demands on an International referee will be more intense). The basic training for aerobic fitness is a 1½-mile run – about seven laps of a rugby field. Aim to run a lap in 80–90 seconds (off a running start), then rest for 4½ minutes before the next one. As you become fitter, reduce the rest period to 3 minutes. This type of running builds up aerobic fitness.

To work on anaerobic fitness, run 55 yards at about 70–80% of your maximum speed. Walk back to give yourself time to recover. Do this eight times before resting for three minutes, then do another set of eight, rest for three minutes, and do a third set of eight. The fitter you get, you might like to consider jogging back instead, which will cut down on the amount of recovery you have and make it that much harder to work. You'll be getting fitter because you need to work, and you have to put in the same amount of work in less time if you want to get progressively fit. Finally, jog two or three laps at a very easy pace to warm down before going in for a very welcome shower and a pint.

It is necessary to retain interest and enthusiasm, so have variety in your training programme. The fast running can be varied with a continuous, flat-out shuttle run of 12 × 5 yards. A shuttle run is when you run from the touch line to the five-metre line, turn, run back to the touch line, turn and so on. Again, rest for three minutes between each set. Another variation is three sets of 12 × 15 yards – not a shuttle run, but a straight and fast run and a walk or jog back. Rest for three minutes between each set.

Your aim should be to work up to a set of 5 × 22 yards, 4 × 40 yards, 3 × 50 yards, 2 × 60 yards and 1 × 75 yards, with a walk-back recovery between each run. We found that there were very few times when a referee had to run more than about 60 or 70 yards, and the majority of the runs were somewhere between 20 and 35 yards.

All training sessions should, of course, be preceded by an adequate warm-up. This should consist of bending and stretching exercises such as standing with your hands holding onto your feet and then straightening your legs. Then do six sets of squat thrusts, press-ups and trunk curls, in each case as many as you can manage in fifteen seconds. The reason for this specific order is that you exercise different muscles and you are able to do the six sets continuously. Never use the weight of the body to increase the range of movement by, for example, bending over and pumping down to try and touch the floor. It's the surest way to tear hamstrings. If you want to warm up first by just doing a little light jogging, that's fine.

Train twice a week during the season, plus the game that you do. I don't think it is necessary to do it more than twice a week in view of the fact that you are refereeing as well and in fact, if you have two games a week, one training session would be enough. It is best, if possible, to train at the time of day when the games might take place, especially in countries with wide temperature and humidity variations, but most people have to fit in training when they can.

The training pattern I have described so far is for use during the season, but it would be wise to follow a year-round routine beginning in May or June (in the northern hemisphere) with two runs a week of two or three miles (preferably on grass) and all the other sports you might care to indulge in: tennis, squash, swimming and so on. Your running will give you your aerobic capacity, but tennis and squash, which are anaerobic exercises, will help in the other part of your programme later on so it is advisable to play these games as well as going for a run. As the season approaches, intersperse your three-mile run with fast runs over irregular distances, along with walking and jogging. There are times when you need to sprint in the game, so you need a degree of strength in order to be able to do that, and you need some explosive quality. Circuit training, better still a little bit of weight training, especially for your legs, will satisfy that demand.

Like any player, if a referee is under par, if he's had flu or he's got a heavy cold, then he shouldn't referee – it's as simple as that. If a referee is injured, especially if he's got a leg injury, considering the amount of running he has to do, it would be very foolish. You might be OK for the first half, but I can well remember a game involving the college at which I teach. The referee came up to me as I stood on the touch line and said, 'Damn, I feel bad, I feel awful, I've had flu all the week. Is there anybody here who can take over? Can you do it?'

I replied, 'Well, it's not fair that I should take over with the College involved,' and the opposition boys said, 'Oh, not him!'

166

Eventually, though, the referee came over and said, 'Look, I've got to go off, I just can't carry on.'

So they rushed me out in wellington boots, a pair of shorts that were too long for me and a mac, and there I was – refereeing in his stead! So if you're not feeling well, then it would not be in your best interests, or the interest of the players, or of the game in general, for you to referee.

Finally, bear in mind that when fatigue sets in, skill breaks down: that's a well-known fact. Skill is about making decisions and that is the referee's job. If you are physically tired you are apt to make errors of judgement and to be less mentally alert, which could be of considerable significance in the final quarter of a fast, close and exciting game. Above all, if you keep fit, the more you will enjoy your refereeing.

20

A National Coaching Scheme

by JOHN DAWES

Having captained London Welsh, Wales and the British Lions during his playing career, John Dawes is now Coaching Organiser to the WRU.

This chapter sets out to explain the coaching scheme which exists here in Wales. However, before attempting to give details of the scheme, it is necessary to have a little of the geographical and cultural background in relation to rugby in Wales. Fig. 29 is a map of the world on which Wales has been pin-pointed to show exactly how small our rugby nation is. Fig. 30 is a map of Wales on which all the Welsh Rugby Union Clubs have been marked, to indicate the concentration of rugby football in South Wales. It also shows that the distances between clubs is relatively small. The rugby geography of Wales therefore enables the administration of the game in Wales to be relatively simple compared to the sizes of other countries. Examining further the situation of the rugby clubs, certain clubs have a special position, mainly established through tradition and not through any rule or bye-law of the WRU. These clubs are those indicated by a ringed dot on Fig. 30. Tradition has it that clubs in the vicinity of these special clubs feed players into them, thereby improving the standard of the major clubs.

Although Wales is obviously a small country, the Welsh people are of a non-nomadic tradition. A Welshman tradition-ally lives and dies in his own village and there is a great tribal influence associated with any village large or small. This pro-duces a different attitude towards various aspects of life whether it is social, cultural, education etc. For example, Ebbw Vale was historically an area of the iron-ore industry, with the clubs down

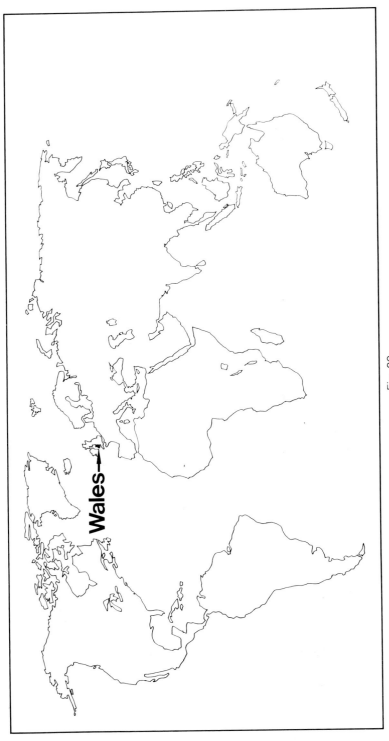

Fig. 29

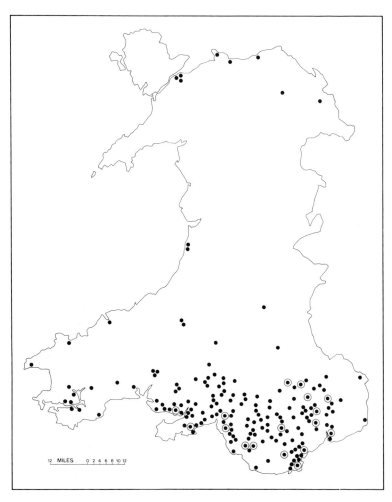

Fig. 30

the Valley to the port of Newport being traditionally coal-
mining. The effect this had on rugby football was that the players
they produced developed into strong, muscular, if somewhat
short, forwards; indeed, the area of Gwent, as it is now called, is
recognised for its forward prowess. The two major cities, Swansea and Cardiff, have a more traditional city environment where
rugby football becomes more of a game and less of an essential

170

ingredient of life than it is in the Valleys. However, being major cities, the attraction to them of general players was such that they have developed into two of the most highly regarded clubs in the world.

Geographically and culturally, therefore, it is obvious that in Wales there is a tradition to the development of the game which automatically brings to the surface top-class players inbred with intense rivalry. That fact alone has helped to explain the success that Wales has achieved on the field of rugby. However, with the development of the game and the visits of other rugby nations to Wales, and Wales to other rugby nations, it soon became obvious that a reliance on these ingredients alone was not enough.

One of Wales' most frustrating periods was between 1951 and 1969 when, although many great individuals were produced – for example Rhys Williams, Roy John, Cliff Morgan, Bleddyn Williams – only one mythical Triple Crown was won. Further, apart from the solitary success against New Zealand in 1953, Wales achieved very little success against other overseas countries during this period. It was Wales' disastrous result against South Africa in Durban in 1964 that precipitated the need for the coaching scheme which is currently in existence. Whilst there is no doubt that before this time 'coaches' did exist, they were not called that and there was certainly no organised coaching taking part in the club structure of Welsh rugby. Although by virtue of the rugby environment in Wales there was a heavy bias in its grammar schools towards rugby football, this was proving to be totally insufficient.

As a result, a small body of men led by Mr Cliff Jones were charged with the responsibility of investigating the organised structure, or lack of it, in Wales at that time. Without doubt, the most significant step that Mr Jones and his Committee recommended was that the WRU should employ a person to be solely responsible for the playing organisation of the game in Wales. Whilst this was of tremendous significance, what was totally fortuitous was that the man appointed to this very responsible position was available: Mr Ray Williams, who is now Secretary of the Welsh Rugby Union. The problems that Mr Williams faced, the hurdles that he had to overcome and the lack of organisation which was so obvious, are now well-known, probably throughout the world of rugby football.

This background will perhaps help you better to understand the scheme which is current in Welsh rugby. The Welsh Rugby Union, like most other Unions, is governed by a Committee

171

which is elected annually. The election of this Committee is solely the responsibility of the clubs. From this Committee is nominated a sub-committee which is known as the Coaching and Laws Committee. As the name implies, they are charged, under the General Committee, with the responsibility for all practical aspects of the game of rugby football. Serving on the Coaching and Laws Committee, Wales are extremely fortunate to have men of the highest rugby calibre, such as Rhys Williams, former International lock-forward, and Hermas Evans, the WRU Representative on the International Board. Servicing this Committee on a professional basis there are two technical men known in the WRU as the Coaching Organiser and the Assistant Coaching Organiser. Their prime responsibility is to implement the decisions of the Coaching and Laws Committee throughout the length and breadth of Wales. Like any civil servant, the Coaching Organiser and the Assistant Coaching Organiser have a duty to keep the Committee well informed of developments, news, recommendations for their consideration etc.

In addition to the Coaching and Laws Committee, the WRU have set up a Coaching Advisory Committee consisting of people who are not necessarily members of the WRU Committee but who have a strong rugby background. They are popularly known as the 'think tank' of Welsh rugby and their task is to analyse certain aspects of the game, leading to significant developments. They have produced papers on:

Back Row Forward Play (1968)
The Lineout (1975)
Back Play (1976)
Pressure on Players (1979).

In the mid-1960s the WRU Committee recommended to its clubs that they should each have a coach, and this led to the development of coaches' courses and a basic scheme of coaching throughout Wales. These courses stress the need for the individual coach to be himself and coach according to his own style and philosophy. It is obvious, however, that there are themes which are common to all. A typical course timetable is on the facing page. One can see from this that all the important aspects of rugby football such as techniques, laws, injuries etc are discussed. As far as possible, all the morning and afternoon practical sessions take place outside.

ASSEMBLE IN LECTURE ROOM AT 9.15 am EACH DAY

Day	9.15 am–12.30 pm	2.15–4.30 pm	Sundowners	7.30 onwards
Saturday		2.15 pm Opening address The concept (theory), followed by: The skills (practical)	Video of skills Seminars	Recreation
Sunday	Basic coaching (practical) Handling, leading to continuity and development of back play; followed by mutual coaching	As morning session	"	The search for fitness
Monday	Basic coaching (practical) Contact and support leading to maul and ruck; followed by mutual coaching	As morning session	"	The art of teaching/ coaching
Tuesday	Basic coaching (practical) Set play for forwards including scrum, lineout and kick-off; followed by mutual coaching	As morning session	"	Injuries in sport
Wednesday	Basic coaching (practical) Team play, incorporating attack and defence	As morning session	"	Mini-Rugby: the game and its objectives
Thursday	The Laws (theory) The Laws (practical) Coaching Assessment 10.30 am–1.00 pm and	Mutual coaching (2½ hours)	"	Coaching Award paper
Friday	Prep Coaching Assessment 10.30 am–1.00 pm and	2.15–4.15 pm	Disperse	

LUNCH AT 1.00 pm

DINNER AT 6.30 pm

In addition to the coaches' courses there is an Annual Coaches' Conference which all those on the Register of Coaches are given an opportunity to attend and which lasts for one weekend. The topics for this coaching weekend are selected by the Coaching and Laws Committee and are always topics which are pertinent to the game at that particular time.

In the Welsh Rugby Union there are three grades of coach. These are:

1 *Coach*, capable of dealing with teams at club or school level.
2 *Senior Coach*, capable of dealing with District and County teams, of instructing on courses for players and of assisting on courses for coaches.
3 *Staff Coach*, capable of coaching at the highest level and of conducting courses for and assessing coaches.

An aspiring coach must attend a course and be assessed at the end of that course. However, the WRU do not believe that a course of one week's duration necessarily makes a man a coach; the course is simply a means of supplying him with the tools of the trade. After successfully completing the course, the individual returns to coaching in a club and within one year, following a satisfactory report from the club itself, he will be listed on the WRU Register of Coaches. Those who fail the week's course are encouraged to obtain more coaching experience and to return to a course at some future date. It is not automatic that a person on the course acquires the status of a WRU coach, since it is important to maintain standards.

WRU coaches who have been with a particular club, school, college etc for a period of four years are eligible for promotion. The procedure is that the club should write to the WRU supplying a confidential report on the coach and indicating that the coach himself is keen for promotion. This report will be considered as an application by the Coaching and Laws Committee. If it is favourably received the Coaching Committee will nominate one or more from the Chairman of the Committee, the Coaching Organiser, the Assistant Coaching Organiser or a Staff Coach to visit the club on a training night and a further report will be submitted to the Coaching and Laws Committee. The Committee will then be in a position to extend an invitation to the nominated coach to become a Senior Coach. Promotion from Senior Coach to Staff Coach is entirely at the discretion of the

Coaching Committee. Clubs can nominate Senior Coaches for promotion to Staff Coaches by means of a confidential letter to the Coaching Committee.

The scheme outlined in this chapter is peculiar to Wales but has been found to be successful. It is hoped that this will help particularly emerging rugby countries to devise a scheme of their own so that ultimately they will produce young men capable of developing the game to the highest level.

21

A National Refereeing Scheme

by SAM WILLIAMS

Sam Williams started his refereeing career in the Newport & District Rugby Union in 1949, passed the WRU examination in 1950 and was included on the official list in 1952. He was Secretary and Chairman of the Gwent Society 1954–60, and was a founder-member of the Welsh Referees' Society. He joined the London Society of Referees in 1961 before returning to Wales in 1968 and retiring in 1974. Since his retirement, he has been fully involved in the administration of refereeing work, acting as an observer and assessor of referees. He has helped to organise and administer the Welsh Rugby Union referees' courses and in the WRU Centenary Year was President of the Welsh Referees' Society.

It is now readily accepted that every national rugby body should be concerned with the performance and therefore the training of its referees. Individual approaches may place different emphasis on different aspects of the training but for the sake of brevity I will be concerned in this chapter only with the situation as it exists in Wales.

After the war, the administrators of the game in Wales closely studied the refereeing situation and generally agreed that to improve the standard, a referee education system needed to be devised and developed. Dedication and experience on their own were not enough: there must also be that advanced level of technical ability and attitude which would ensure that the individual referee's performances were brought to a new level, in keeping with the development of the modern game. Initially the three main aims were:

1 To improve the standard of refereeing at all levels in Wales from beginner to International level;
2 To provide all potential referees with the necessary basics and the best type of instruction available in the laws of the game;
3 In so doing, to increase the incentives for ex-players to become referees.

Twenty years later, as a result of experience and in order to achieve these aims, two major further objectives were set:

1 A basis for a national course of theoretical and practical training to be given for referees, with the accent on the practical training;
2 A standardised scheme of accreditation through a system of examinations and grading.

The role of the Welsh Rugby Union has been to organise, administer and evaluate all the courses. Before 1960, the Union paid only modest attention to its referees, being responsible just for the setting and organisation of examinations as a means of securing an adequate supply of referees of a minimum standard of ability. With the appointment in the early 1960s of a Coaching Organiser and later an Assistant Coaching Organiser, much more thought was given to the training of referees. There was increased interest in catering for referees, parallel with the great push forward in the establishment of a coaches' scheme. The professional staff dealing with both schemes came to their new posts with wide experience of rugby coaching but did not claim to have equal experience of refereeing. It is to their credit that they have applied themselves to the understanding of refereeing problems and needs and have been largely responsible in advising their Committees on new approaches to be tried in the training, examining and grading of referees. When such schemes were adopted, they have also supervised and monitored each development.

Back in the 1940s and 1950s the Welsh Rugby Union set standards by examining potential referees at written and oral examinations. Candidates who gave enough correct answers were included in due course on an official list of WRU referees as vacancies on that list occurred. Priority was given to referees nominated or promoted by Junior, Youth or School Unions, and there was a flavour of patronage about the whole thing.

As years went by, there were refinements to the types of question asked in these examinations and much greater thought was given to the preparation of intending referees through the medium of pre-examination courses. These were a series of theoretical lectures and discussions held at venues throughout Wales, where the laws were discussed and interpretations given by the lecturer in charge. Clearly, this was a big step forward in the preparation of referees but it still did nothing more than take a fairly academic approach to their training. These pre-examination courses were sometimes used to obtain a feed-back from the lecturers and the candidates and, as a result of such feed-back, the Welsh Rugby Union adopted a more constructive format for the lectures, requiring a greater emphasis on dealing with practical situations rather than on endless academic discussions. The next stage followed very quickly and certain centres in Wales were allowed, even encouraged, to add practical sessions to their theoretical courses at the discretion of local lecturers. There was an immediate and dramatic response from lecturers and students in the form of clear demands for more practical work. This in turn led to a new format which married the two elements of theory and practice and became six two-hour sessions in a lecture room, undertaken over a three-week period, together with a full day's practical course where set pieces were set up and examined in detail, using the students themselves both as players and as referees in charge.

At this time, and outside the direction of the Welsh Rugby Union, some experiments were being carried out by interested individuals acting on behalf of local referees' societies, who were themselves becoming more active in their discussions at meetings and showed much greater concern than they had done previously in improving the performance of young referees. Such experiments were held at club training sessions or at junior games, where a senior referee would give specific instructions on what he was looking for and so on. Experiments were done with shadow refereeing, in which a senior referee would work with a junior referee, moving from place to place together. I have known of such shadow refereeing involving six students trooping along behind a senior referee in order to cover all the possible eventualities. Other experiments included teach-ins where small groups of referees looked at specific areas of work, limiting themselves to scrummages or lineouts, rucks and mauls and so on, and discussing their findings later. There were stop and start sessions where the directing referee stopped the game and explained the decisions as they were given by him. I was involved myself in one experiment where a two-way radio was tried – I am glad to say that this particular idea was abandoned.

The discussions which took place at the final sessions of Welsh Rugby Union courses all pointed towards the students' preference for more and more practical experience in game situations, in a concentrated and constructive fashion. The problems of having insufficient players available as guinea pigs for all these various courses caused many problems for organisers and eventually focussed on a need to rationalise the situation. This led to the consideration of one- or two-day courses in a limited number of centres. This was tried and used for a few years with a fairly large number of course venues for the theoretical work feeding into a smaller number of centres concentrating on practical work. It was possible in this way to use the limited number of International referees at every practical course, thus ensuring that all the students got the same information from the same sources.

The next stage continued to recognise the increasing need for practical work, the use of a few top referees only and the desire to concentrate the course within a fixed time-limit. Thus the fragmented courses throughout Wales were replaced, experimentally, by one residential course at the National Sports Centre in Cardiff. The response was terrific: nearly 100 enrolled on this first course which ran from Friday evening until Sunday evening. The course programme still recognised the need for theoretical instruction but was able to increase the amount of practical work that could be done and included such useful ancillaries as expert information on first-aid and fitness training, as well as syndicate discussions and practical refereeing situations. Since then, the time allowed for the theoretical discussion of laws and other ancillary topics has been steadily reduced and the practical time increased. A typical format might be:

1   Introductory section after arrival, dealing with:
    (a)   The WRU Training Scheme and Welsh Society of Referees
    (b)   The philosophy and attitudes of referees
    (c)   Fitness for referees
    (d)   First-aid for referees

(e) Cameos and problem areas
(f) Films and other visual aids.

2 The main programme, dealing with practical demonstrations
and involving the students in game situations:

(a) Set pieces – scrum, lineout, ruck and maul, kick-offs,
penalty kicks
(b) Open play including obstruction, static and moving
situations, off-side and on-side
(c) The observation of a practical team coaching session
(d) The observation of International referees in charge of a
game.

This section to emphasise again the practical nature of the
course, with as little talking in these practical sessions as
possible. The students to learn by seeing and doing.

3 Each practical session to be followed by separate syndicate
discussions which themselves explore the points of law and
interpretation and provide a feed-back to the general body of
the course. The same approach to be taken regarding com-
ments on the course in general at the end of the last session, to
possible improvements in the course.

Clearly, these courses must aim at consistency rather than
uniformity or stereotyping. Each must have a rational structure,
with a co-ordinated approach, and must highlight those key
factors which represent the most desirable elements in good
referees. This is not an exhaustive list, but those factors would
include:

Competence
Control
Consistency
Courage
Integrity and understanding
Respect
Enjoyment
Fitness

The advantages of the present system may be listed as:

1 It increases the competence of referees
2 It sets standards of knowledge and ability which will ultimately improve the status of referees

3   It encourages players intending to become referees and improves, progressively, their refereeing knowledge
4   It improves the flow of information to referees
5   It rationalises the preparation and education of referees
6   It effects economics and simplifies the educational approach to the training of referees
7   It is a common point of reference for referees and administrators in the game.

Some of its disadvantages are:

1   Its fixed venue and date rule out some people from joining
2   It requires a three-day commitment
3   There is no alternative passage to the WRU examination
4   It requires large facilities to cope with the numbers.

There are no plans by the WRU radically to change the present national training scheme. It is time now for a period of consolidation during which to evaluate the benefits of their practical approach. However, my personal belief is that this concentrated weekend national course should be supplemented by a system of preparation discussions which will ensure that referees come to the course with an improved knowledge of the laws. This does not mean that we need the full series of theoretical discussions that we had at one time, and it may be that the responsibility for providing such introductions to refereeing could be the responsibility of district referees' societies. The societies would welcome the opportunities to be involved and it may be that such involvement would lead to a much closer integration between those concerned with the improvement of what is already considered to be very good potential material for refereeing.

Already, the monthly meetings of each district referees' society provide another very important area for training referees. A great deal of their time is spent in discussing the laws and their interpretation. Most societies arrange to have a member who will lead the discussion, having prepared a topic, and this may sometimes result in differences of opinion which cannot be resolved at district level. When this happens, interpretations are sought from the parent referee body, the Welsh Society of Referees, which has its own Laws Committee of about nine people (which includes all the International referees). Interpretations agreed by that Committee are then transmitted back to all the district societies, not only to the district from which the referral came. It is accepted that such interpretations are binding on all Welsh referees. If the Society's Laws Committee is itself unable to come to an agreed decision or requires further consultation, it will refer the matter to the Laws Sub-Committee of the Welsh Rugby Union for decision. One of the most helpful things as far as Welsh referees are concerned is that the International referees are able to report back very quickly on any agreed interpretations at International Board level. This ensures that all referees are in communication with the top levels of decision-making and no time is lost in waiting for them to filter through the administration.

Additionally, the Welsh Rugby Union has in recent years organised a biennial national conference of Welsh referees. The structured programmes have included discussions on the problem areas of law interpretation and the operations of member referees. Referees of eminence from various countries have been invited to address the conferences on selected topics, and although such national conferences are, of course, open only to referees who are on the Welsh Union list, it may be that in due course it will be possible to open them up for all referees at all levels.

The international exchange of ideas is also welcomed by all Welsh referees and they would fully support any decision to hold more frequently events like the WRU Centenary International Conference for Coaches and Referees; it is seen as another stage in the training of referees.

Grading referees
It should not be thought that the responsibility of the Welsh Rugby Union in training referees begins and ends with courses. Indeed, it could be said that the courses themselves are only the first stage in training referees, and they are followed up by a system of grading on a two-tier system. This applies both to referees on the official list of the Welsh Rugby Union and to those working in district unions who have passed the written and oral examinations of the Union.

The first part of the two-tier system is each rugby club forwarding a report on the referee after every match, indicating simply, on a score scale between one and nine, where the club places that referee in comparison with its other visiting referees. This information is fed into a computer which with due allowance for any bias enables a reasonable comparative print-out to be obtained on all referees. This is supported by an organised system of observation wherein selected referees from each of the grades, 1–4, and the probationary referees of course, are looked at and observers' written reports are sent to the Union which uses them to supplement the information obtained by the club card system. The Welsh Rugby Union considers that the observers do a very important job and I would emphasise that the observers have probationary referees as their top priority. These are given advice and encouragement as well as being assessed. The observers point out in the early stages of a referee's career where improvements should be made and attention is drawn to any problem areas in the interpretation of laws and so forth. Their second priority is to look at referees who may be moving up or down between grades. This enables a referee's grade to be confirmed. Thirdly, in order to improve the standards of the grades, selected referees are looked at from each grade. Lastly, from time to time there are specific referrals for one reason or another.

There are between 140 and 150 referees operating at Welsh Rugby Union matches. At the very top level, of course, there are half-a-dozen referees, some of whom are on the International panel and others on the exchange list. In that same grade there are 17 or 18 other referees, making a total of about 24, who will generally be allocated to handle the first-class matches. There are between 20 and 22 referees in Grade 2 and they will also, from time to time, referee the important matches. Grade 3 will have a much bigger number, between 40 and 44, and referee the large bulk of Welsh Rugby Union fixtures. Grade 4, which is the beginner level, will have about 40 referees and they cover the remaining matches. Lastly, there will be about 20 probationary referees each year who will be seen by assessors during the season prior to their acceptance on the WRU list.

I am fully committed to the concept of a national training scheme for referees and am convinced that it must be done through practical teaching methods. My two main areas of concern for the future reflect the increasing pressures of the fast modern game and the frailty of referees who will control it, and in writing about them I am doing so in a personal capacity and putting forward my own opinions.

The last re-write of the laws of the game caused it to be dramatically speeded up. It put new demands on players in terms of fitness, and in most clubs there is an established regime of regular fitness training sessions at which all the players have to conform to the set pattern. I would ask that more attention is paid by the National Unions to advising referees on fitness and by referees to preparing themselves better for the game. We should not forget that the fit, alert referee is an asset to the game while the slow and unfit referee is a hindrance to it.

At present the compulsory retirement age for WRU referees on the list is 50. This does not mean that 50-year-olds have to stop operating as there are no such age barriers in the junior levels of the game. However, I believe that the physical demands on referees will increase with the speed of the game and that thought should be given to reducing the retiring age to a more realistic one of 45. There will be many referees who would plead that they are in the prime of life and fit to continue beyond this age and I would not deny them the opportunity to do so. They would be invaluable for junior and school matches, where the players should benefit from the attentions of experienced referees. Neither personal ambitions to control top-class matches, nor the view that reversion to youth matches would be down-grading, should be allowed to colour the principles involved.

If the retirement age were set at 45, then the WRU would need to reconsider the effective life of a referee on its list and probably set an age limit for referees going on that list. Anything less than five years would not be worthwhile and thought would need to be given to the Union's investment in referees' courses. It would not make much sense to invite new referees onto the national training course if they were older than 37 or 38. An upper age limit of 35 could be set on referees attending the course so that nine or ten years refereeing on the list would be possible.

Rugby is still a young man's game and we should recognise that fact for referees as well as for players. Would not such a move also be more likely to attract ex-players to refereeing in recognition of the emphasis on youth and fitness? Would it not give referees a better chance of being fair to the players, being fair to themselves and their fellow referees, and of giving of their best to the game they love?

Afterword

by RAY WILLIAMS

*Ray Williams was Coaching Organiser for the
WRU 1976–79, Deputy Secretary and Centenary
Officer 1979–81, and is now Secretary.*

In the early 1970s I began to have visions of the future: of a Welsh
Rugby Union Centenary season which did not stop at celebratory
matches; of a Centenary which had as one of its objectives that of
making a contribution to the development of the game throughout the world. I have always felt very strongly that the International Board countries have a great responsibility to ensure that
the game progresses throughout the world in a way which is
totally acceptable and in keeping with its long-established tradi-
tions. One thing is certain: such development will not just
happen. It will only be realised as the result of positive action.

There were those, of course, who thought that my dreams
were either delusions of grandeur, pie in the sky or a combination
of both! Such negative thinking did not deter me. In seeking to
establish coaching as an essential part of the game I had come
across tougher problems and was convinced that I would have the
support of my Union, whose record of encouragement to the
emerging Rugby nations was second to none. My optimism was
justified and the WRU agreed that an International Conference
of Coaches and Referees should be an integral part of the WRU
Centenary programme. This involved a very heavy financial
commitment, but substantial financial support from Adidas and
Umbro International, together with the Sports Council for
Wales, helped to make a dream a reality.

This book is the practical legacy of that unique gathering of
coaches and referees from some forty-seven rugby-playing countries. It recounts accurately the philosophies, thoughts and ideas
of some of the world's great rugby technicians. What it cannot do
is encapsulate the great feeling that the Conference generated;
neither can it depict the hopes, needs and ambitions of those
who wish desperately to become part of the Rugby brother-
hood. In this latter respect, before people start criticising the

185

International Rugby Football Board, it ought to be realised that the Board has no mandate to organise Rugby throughout the world. Its present functions are to produce the laws of the game, to define the rules on amateurism and to arrange a schedule of international fixtures. One effect of the Conference has been for the Board to look very closely at its constitution and now a committee has been set up to examine the Board's role in the game. An early recommendation of this committee which has been accepted by the Board is that conferences such as that held in Cardiff in September 1980 will now be held at regular intervals.

I always felt that in the final analysis the International Conference of Coaches and Referees would turn out to be the most significant event of the WRU Centenary Year. I see no reason to change that judgement. In fact, the publication of this book supports it. I hope by reading it that those lucky enough to be present in Cardiff will recapture the spirit of a remarkable ten days, and that the book will add to the game's thinking and knowledge.

Appendix

It was the wish of the Conference to present to the WRU firm recommendations which, if approved, they would in turn present to the International Board.
The main recommendations fall into three categories:

A Injuries in rugby football
B Violence in rugby football
C The future of International Board and emerging countries

INJURIES IN RUGBY FOOTBALL

The Conference was of the opinion that many injuries which occur in either the playing of rugby football, or the practice of training for rugby football, were caused by factors other than those which involved transgressing the laws.
Some of the major reasons given were:

(a) A lack of fitness and body conditioning, ie. fitness and conditioning specific to a particular position, eg. front-row forwards.
(b) A poor technique, due to lack of knowledge and understanding by the individual player, or indeed lack of proper and adequate instruction.
(c) The laws, which should be looked at from the point of view of the physical demands and pressures the game places upon the body. If statistics prove it to be necessary, then laws should be amended.
(d) Deliberate transgression of the laws. This falls into two categories:
   (i)   those transgressions which lead to a technical and hence physical advantage;
   (ii) those transgressions which involve or lead to foul play.

The Conference recommended:

1   More research should be done on the fitness needs of the players and how they can achieve acceptable standards of fitness without adding to their already heavy commitments. Players who are unfit should not participate in the playing of the game. This should include players who are either unfit, returning too soon after injury or coming out of retirement to play.

2   Proper teaching and application of correct technique is a factor which prevents injury. Wrong or dangerous techniques must be discouraged. Players must be made aware of the inherent danger of poor technique. Coaches and players, especially at top level, have an obligation to set the highest standards of behaviour, attitude and technique. The influence on senior players is profound as techniques are imitated by younger and less skilful players. Dubious techniques can therefore be a source of danger.

3   Referees are asked to enforce the laws strictly, especially those which could lead to injury.

4   A medical survey, similar to that carried out in New Zealand, should be undertaken to obtain all possible information on all the factors that contribute to injuries within the game.

VIOLENCE IN RUGBY FOOTBALL

In the teaching of and coaching of players, especially the young, the highest standards must be stressed. Much is written about the 'spirit of the game' but it was strongly suggested that the International Board should publish a Code of Conduct which would be universally accepted.

Included in such a code could be:

(a)   Players must be encouraged to use more self-discipline.

(b)   The unlawful use of physical force should be severely dealt with, ie. the referee must send off the offender (no previous warning needed).

(c)   Stricter and longer terms of suspension should be imposed.

(d)   Players known to be serious offenders should be banned from playing for any club in a Union by that Union's governing body.

(e)   Some form of 'sin-bin', as in ice hockey, ought to be tried.

Because of the areas of doubt surrounding these aspects a certain conditioned and physical style of rugby, not shared with non-IB countries, has developed. This, of course, is not conducive to the world-wide development of the game.

FUTURE DEVELOPMENT OF THE GAME

All delegates agreed that:

(a) The experience of sharing with all rugby countries was very worthwhile and must be continued.
(b) The inter-relationship between referees and coaches *must* be encouraged and strengthened.
(c) Communication is vital between *all* countries.

The Conference would wish and strongly recommend that:

1   The IB take the initiative and hold similar world conferences on a regular basis, eg. every four years. Such conferences need not necessarily be held in IB member-countries only.
2   The IB again take the initiative and establish a formal structure by which all rugby-playing countries are considered to be affiliated to members of the IB. This body to meet regularly to recommend changes and be consulted on all critical issues relating to the game.
3   The IB direct one member union to act as a clearing-house for information and co-ordinator of requests for technical assistance in the years when no conference is held. These terms to be held for two years and that initially the WRU to be asked to act in this capacity.
4   A form of register of individual coaches and referees be established for the information of all playing countries.